Lighthouse Ghosts

13 bona fide apparitions standing watch over America's shores

by Norma Elizabeth
Photographs by Bruce Roberts

CRANE HILL
PUBLISHERS

Published by Crane Hill Publishers
www.cranehill.com

Printed in the United States of America

Cover photo: Outer Island Light Station, on one of the 22 Apostle Islands in
              Lake Superior off the coast of Wisconsin.

Library of Congress Cataloging-in-Publication Data

Elizabeth, Norma, 1947-
Lighthouse ghosts / by Norma Elizabeth and Bruce Roberts.
p.   cm.
Includes bibliographical references.
ISBN-13: 978157587-0922
ISBN-10: 1-57587-092-4 (TP)
1. Ghosts—United States. 2. Lighthouses—United States. 3. Haunted places—
United States. I. Roberts, Bruce, 1930- II. Title.
GR105.E45 1998
398.2'0973'05—DC21
98-45406
                                                              CIP

We dedicate this book to

Emma, Mimi, and Lois, my lighthouse traveling companions,
—Norma Elizabeth

Marion Stuart McNally Roberts,
—Bruce Roberts

Other books by Bruce Roberts

Lighthouse Families, Cheryl Shelton-Roberts and Bruce Roberts
American Lighthouses, Ray Jones and Bruce Roberts
California Lighthouses, Bruce Roberts and Ray Jones
Eastern Great Lakes Lighthouses, Bruce Roberts and Ray Jones
Mid-Atlantic Lighthouses, Bruce Roberts and Ray Jones
New England Lighthouses, Bruce Roberts and Ray Jones
Southern Lighthouses, Bruce Roberts and Ray Jones
Pacific Northwest Lighthouses, Bruce Roberts and Ray Jones
Western Great Lakes Lighthouses, Bruce Roberts and Ray Jones
Plantation Homes of the James River Bruce Roberts and Elizabeth Kedash

Table of Contents

Acknowledgments

For sharing their personal stories and information about "their" lighthouses, we say a very special thank you to David Ball, Douglas Bingham, Cullen Chambers, Jim Claflin, Marilyn Fischer, John Gale, Jeff and Linda Gamble, Allan Goddard, Celeste Halsema, Tim Harrison, Mike and Carol Korgan, Lynn Morris, Lorraine Parris, Lee Radzak, Avonda Rehs, Rand Shackleton, Nancy and Larry Schnider, Bob and Sandra Shanklin, Nadine and Jerry Tugel, David Wadsworth, and Anne Webster-Wallace.

We also thank Ellen Sullivan for her support and encouragement with this project.

Introduction

Lighthouse keepers took their jobs seriously—VERY seriously.

Each of them swore an oath to keep the light in their tower burning no matter what, and each of them knew that they personally bore the awesome responsibility for the safety of countless ships' crews and passengers. Mariners counted on the keepers to provide a light or sound a fog signal to warn them away from underwater obstacles and to guide them into safe harbor.

From the late 1700s until the last tower was fully automated and unmanned in the 1960s, hundreds of dedicated men, women, and their children worked twenty-four hours a day, seven days a week to keep the lamps in our nation's lighthouses burning. Every evening right after sunset the keepers climbed the narrow spiral staircase inside the tower all the way to the lantern room at the top. The staircases in many towers consisted of uneven, open steps with no handrail—work conditions that would never pass today's occupational safety standards.

Throughout the night the keepers kept checking the lamp to ensure the flame was burning brightly. Every morning just after dawn they extinguished the flame, refilled the lamp with oil or kerosene, trimmed the wick, and cleaned the soot off the lantern room windows and the myriad prisms of the lens. It was a never-ending cycle of climbing, filling, trimming, and cleaning—and that was just to take care of the lamp and lens!

During stormy weather there was no rest for the weary—the keepers or members of their families had to keep the light burning and sometimes sound the fog signal around the clock while continually searching the churning waters for ships in distress. Many lighthouse children, some of them barely in their teens, pitched in during times of crisis to carry heavy cans of fuel up one-unsteady-footstep-and-you-fall staircases, to rotate the lens by hand when the clockwork mechanism broke, and even to row a lifeboat through mountainous waves to rescue shipwreck victims.

The keepers also had to keep up with routine maintenance and repairs on the tower, the lamp and lens, the keeper's dwelling, the outbuildings, the grounds, the lifesaving boat, and every other piece of government-issued property at the light station. And just to make sure the keepers and their families were doing their jobs *right,* an official lighthouse inspector would pop in every once in a while for a surprise visit, perhaps hoping to find a bed unmade or a trace of tarnish on a brass instrument.

The men, women, and children who lived at light stations daily faced the life-giving—and life-taking—forces of nature: winds strong enough to blow a child off a cliff, waves high enough to wash over the top of the tower and dwelling, storms powerful enough to break the glass windows in the lantern room, wash away the soil around the foundation, and sometimes topple the lighthouse itself. Keepers and their families also faced the emotional and psychological demands of isolation: living in remote outposts miles from civilization, days away from medical help, having to make do with available resources or do without. They constantly faced life and death situations, and they often had to dig deep within themselves to overcome fear and pain. Their daily accomplishments are legendary.

After working through such incredible hardships and taking their jobs so seriously, is it any wonder that some of these totally committed, utterly responsible men, women, and children would continue to remain on the job? As one keeper declared when he was forced to retire at age eighty-seven: "I am not going to leave this building!"

Stories about lighthouse ghosts abound—perhaps with good reason. The people who lived and worked at light stations had strong wills, incredible courage, and tremendous inner strength. They waged almost daily battle with the raw forces of nature, they routinely put their lives on the line to save others, and when death came, it often came violently—by drowning, fire, or fatal accident. The spirits of these almost-superhuman people understandably might linger at "their" lighthouse, especially if they felt they had somehow shirked their duty or left before they had completed their assignment. Although the "ghosts" of some keepers, members of their families, and shipwreck victims can be explained as the result of very natural phenomenon, others remain unexplained despite intense scientific investigation.

Whether or not you believe in ghosts, you have to agree that the keepers' spirit of courage, self-sacrifice, and pride in a job well done continues to live on in the lighthouses they served, and that spirit is worth preserving and honoring. That's why lighthouse aficionados are working so hard to save and restore light stations across the United States, historic structures that have been left far too long to the destructive ravages of wind, waves, and vandals. These dedicated volunteer and professional preservationists are also working hard to collect the personal stories of the keepers and their families, so that all of us can have the opportunity to learn what it was like to keep the lights burning in our nation's lighthouses.

Some preservation groups have restored towers and keepers' dwellings and opened them to the public as living-history museums. You can walk where the keepers walked and see objects that were part of their daily lives at Split Rock Lighthouse in Minnesota, St. Augustine and Old Port Boca Grande Lighthouses in Florida, and Old Presque Isle Lighthouse in Michigan. Other preservationists have opened restored towers and dwellings for overnight guests. You can sleep in the keeper's bedroom and have a meal in the dwelling's kitchen at Heceta Head Lighthouse in Oregon and at Big Bay Point in Michigan. Other groups are scrambling to raise funds to save an endangered lighthouse from the wrecking ball or, as with Cape Hatteras, from the ocean itself.

We hope this book will entice you to visit these and other lighthouses. We invite you to climb the stairs in restored towers, inspect the Fresnel lenses in restored lantern rooms, step out onto the catwalks and scan the horizon for passing ships, and spend some time—perhaps even the night—in a keeper's dwelling. We also invite you to support and share in the work of preserving these historic structures so future generations can also experience firsthand what it was like to live and work at a light station, a proud vocation that is fast fading from sight and memory.

As the preservationists at Split Rock Light Station put it, we invite you and your children and your children's children to "explore life in the past lane."

Norma Elizabeth

Norma Elizabeth

Like the lighthouse keeper at Split Rock Lighthouse on Lake Superior near Two Harbors, Minnesota, many keepers were required to live precariously perched high above the sea. For them—as well as for those they protected—the threat of death was constant.

Serving to protect sea travelers, the lighthouse keeper diligently worked to provide a haven for those who were lost or shipwrecked. Some dedicated lighthouse keepers continue to "maintain" their lighthouses even after death.

Lighthouse Ghosts

13 bona fide apparitions standing
watch over America's shores

The light in Old Presque Isle Lighthouse comes on every night—even though there is no electricity or any other source of light in the tower. The U.S. Coast Guard lists it as an "unidentified" light. Lorraine Parris prefers to call it a "spirit" light.

The Spirit Light Shines On

Old Presque Isle Lighthouse on Lake Huron in Presque Isle, Michigan

Keeper George Parris and his wife, Lorraine, spent fourteen happy years together at Old Presque Isle Lighthouse. The lighthouse, built in 1840 at the north end of Presque Isle Harbor, had been decommissioned for about a century when the retired couple took up summer residence in the keeper's dwelling. They opened the grounds and tower to visitors each day from mid-May to mid-October, the shipping season when freighters can travel Lake Huron without the threat of ice clogging the channels.

Lorraine says the cozy restored dwelling was their honeymoon cottage. And what a perfectly lovely place to honeymoon. This secluded outpost about halfway up the Lake Huron coastline of Presque Isle peninsula is very quiet and peaceful. "It's heaven," says Lorraine. "I love being here."

Since the lighthouse no longer served as an active guide to navigation, George and Lorraine didn't have to do the usual keeper's chores of cleaning the Fresnel lens in the tower or making sure the light stayed lit all night and in stormy weather. The Old Presque Isle tower had been dark since the end of the 1870 shipping season when the much taller new Presque Isle Light Station, about a mile north, was completed. The abandoned Old Presque Isle Lighthouse property suffered from neglect until the S.J. Stebbins family, from Lansing, Michigan, bought it from the U.S. government in the early 1900s.

The family rebuilt the 1840 keeper's dwelling and used it as their summer home. They also restored the 30-foot tower, including placing the salvaged lantern room from South Fox Island Lighthouse on top to replace the original lantern room that was removed years earlier. The replacement lantern room held a rotating fourth-order Fresnel lens lit by an electric bulb. Occasionally, the Stebbins family would turn on the light, even though the U.S. Coast Guard considered it a non-charted light and therefore illegal to operate because it might confuse mariners.

Each summer hundreds of tourists drove up the dirt road to the restored Old Presque Isle Lighthouse and requested permission to climb the tower. In the mid-1950s, after the Stebbins children had grown up and the family no longer used the keeper's dwelling on a regular basis, they decided to give in to the tourists. The family left the tower and the dwelling, including the period furnishings from their antique collection, in the hands of caretakers and opened the property to the public as a living-history museum.

George, a retired electrician, and Lorraine became the caretakers of Old Presque Isle Lighthouse and Museum in 1977. They moved into the keeper's dwelling in mid-May and spent every day for the next five months welcoming people from all over the world to the light station. They told them about the lighthouse itself, the keepers who had kept the light burning in the historic tower when it was in active service, ships that had sunk in the area, and the maritime artifacts displayed in the dwelling and on the grounds.

George especially enjoyed entertaining the children who came to the light station. He would lead groups up the circular hand-hewn stone staircase inside the tower and help them climb up the short ladder the last few feet up to the lantern room. He would show them the prisms in the Fresnel lens and tell them how the lens in a working lighthouse turned and flashed its beam over the water. He would take them through the glass doors onto the catwalk and point to freighters gliding across the blue waters of Lake Huron. Then he would help them down the wedge-shaped steps, making sure they didn't fall off the open side of the spiral staircase, and they would ring the huge 3,400-pound bell at the foot of the tower. George would tell them that the sailors on the big ships on the lake could hear the bell ring and feel the vibrations it sent through the water.

George also enjoyed playing pranks on the light station visitors—the grownups as well as the children—by giving them a "muscle test" with the foghorn. The blast of the foghorn invariably knocked the visitors off their feet!

Despite his sometimes embarrassing tricks, everybody loved George, even the creatures that lived in the woods behind the light station. Lorraine recalls watching—from a safe distance—while George coaxed a porcupine to come close enough to be petted. Lorraine says that porcupine even let George pull its tail.

In 1991 a bear decided to hang around the lighthouse grounds. George named the bear Bruno and
used to talk to it. But when Bruno started scaring away
the deer and other creatures and coming too close to
the keeper's dwelling, George told the bear to leave—
and it did!

Every evening after George and Lorraine said good-
bye to the last visitor and locked the tower, they would
sit on the front porch or inside the comfortable living
room, perhaps in front of a cheerful fire in the huge
stone fireplace, and listen to the soothing rhythm of
the water lapping against the pebbled shore. Lorraine
says the waves would lullaby them to sleep each night.
When the colder temperatures of mid-October signaled
the coming of winter's ice on the lake and the end of
the shipping/tourist season, George and Lorraine
would close up their honeymoon cottage and move
back to their winter home closer to the mainland.

On January 2, 1992, George died of a massive heart
attack. The following May, Lorraine didn't want to go
back to their honeymoon cottage alone, but her kids
talked her into it. One evening when Lorraine was
driving along Grand Lake Road on her way back to the
light station, she felt her eyes drawn to the tower—and
to her utter amazement, she saw a light shining in the
lantern room! She knew that wasn't possible because
the electricity to the tower had been cut off in 1979
when someone in the Stebbins family had inadvertently flipped on the switch to the tower light. The lighthouse had flashed its illegal beam across Lake Huron
for about four hours before George and Lorraine
returned from an evening outing, saw the light rotating
in the tower, and immediately shut it off. The next

morning George had disconnected the electricity to the tower, so the light couldn't be turned on again. And to make doubly sure the illegal flashing beacon wouldn't be seen again, coastguardsmen had removed the gears, so the lens could no longer rotate.

As Lorraine drove along that night in May 1992, keeping one eye on the road and the other on the lighthouse, she noticed that the light periodically disappeared—making it appear to be the beam from a rotating beacon. She looked up at the tower when she got back to the lighthouse, but she couldn't see any light in the lantern room from any spot on the light station grounds. The next day she climbed up to the lantern room to reassure herself that no one had reconnected the power lines or put a bulb in the empty socket.

Although Lorraine was relieved that no one had reconnected the electricity or replaced the bulb, she was still concerned about seeing the light the night before. She didn't say anything to anybody about seeing the light for a long time for fear of being ridiculed, but she continued to notice it whenever she drove along the stretch of Grand Lake Road that looks out over Presque Isle Harbor toward the lighthouse. Finally, she mentioned it to members

When you visit Old Presque Isle Lighthouse, climb up to the lantern room and examine the Fresnel lens and empty electric socket. After dark, walk out onto the pier and see the "spirit" light for yourself.

of her family. They were skeptical until they too saw the light. They noticed that the light had a yellow glow, like the light from an oil lamp rather than the white light of an electric bulb. And when they used high-powered binoculars, they could make out a shadowy figure, sometimes in the lantern room and sometimes on the catwalk.

Gradually, the word spread, and soon people began gathering nightly with their binoculars on Grand Lake Road as well as on the marina pier at Presque Isle Harbor. Boaters close to shore as well as freighters miles out on the lake reported being able to see the light. National Guard pilots reported seeing it when they flew night missions over the peninsula. And the U.S. Coast Guard began taking notice of it, too.

In August some coast guardsmen came to the light station and told Lorraine that she had to turn off the illegal light. She told them that she "would be glad to turn it off if they could tell her how it comes on!" The men dutifully checked to make sure there was no power going to the electrical socket inside the Fresnel lens. They changed the direction of the lens, and they conducted extensive tests, including ordering all the lights in the area (even New Presque Isle Lighthouse a mile up the road) to remain dark for a period of time one night. But they could not come up with an explanation for what was making the light—or a way to keep it from coming on.

The light "still comes on every night as regular as a clock," says Lorraine. "It comes on at dusk and goes off at daylight." The U.S. Coast Guard has classified it as an "unidentified" light. Lorraine prefers to call it a "spirit" light.

Since the light first came on in early 1992, a number of boaters have taken the time to come to Old Presque Isle Lighthouse and thank Lorraine for having the light in the tower. One girl told her that a she and her friends had been out on the lake the night before and couldn't see their way in the fog. "We did some awful tall praying," the girl told Lorraine, "because we didn't know where we were—we didn't have any idea where we were." All of a sudden "a light seemed to appear, and we started following it," the girl reported. "Pretty soon we stopped the boat and looked up, and the light stopped. We started up the boat again, and the light led us right into the harbor. When we got into the harbor, there was no more fog, and the light was gone."

Everybody who knew George when he was alive "figures that it's George up there" turning on the light, says Lorraine. "He's an electrician, and who else would know how to turn on the light except God and an electrician!"

On July 4, 1992, family members gathered at Old Presque Isle Lighthouse for a picnic. When one of the women took her little girl up to the top of the tower to watch the fireworks, the girl started crying and refused to go up into the lantern room. She told her mother that there was a man standing at the top of the stairs. Her mother didn't see anyone, but she took the frightened girl back down the steps. After the girl quieted down, her mother asked her what the man looked like. The little girl said he was tall, had snow-white hair and a beard, and wore glasses. This was a good description of George, who had passed away before the little girl had met him. When the little girl saw a picture of

George later, she said he was the man in the tower, only he had been "brighter white" when she saw him than he was in the picture.

Video artist Rand Shackleton featured Old Presque Isle Lighthouse in *Great Lakes Lighthouses: Shining Through* (Volume One). When he was filming at the light station, he asked Lorraine what it was like to have the unidentified light in the tower. Lorraine replied, "I feel like it's a protection."

Sometimes she feels George in the dwelling with her. She recalls waking up some mornings smelling eggs and sausage cooking—a familiar aroma since that's what George used to cook for her for breakfast every morning.

Lorraine knows that George was with her at the light station September 5, 1992, when a violent thunderstorm was brewing. She tried to go out the back door of the dwelling to get to her car, but someone had moved the round white metal table and two chairs smack dab in front of the screen door, and she couldn't push it open. "It was as if someone was sitting in the chair and pushing back against the door. I couldn't budge it," says Lorraine. And it's a good thing she couldn't—if she had gone out the back door at that time she would have been struck by the lightning bolt that hit a minute later exactly where she would have been standing. The bolt was so powerful it knocked the surge protector right out of its socket under the living room window. Lorraine will always be grateful for the someone who prevented her from getting out the back door that stormy day.

One evening some coast guardsmen came to visit Lorraine. After reminiscing about George and talking about the spirit light, one of them asked Lorraine if she thought George would like to have a shot of whiskey. She told them that he used to enjoy a drink, and she climbed up the tower to the lantern room with the men where they filled a shot glass and left it for George. After they had descended the stairs, Lorraine locked the tower as she does every night.

First thing the next morning she climbed up to the lantern room to retrieve the shot glass before any visitors arrived. She could smell the liquor from the night before, but she could not find the shot glass anywhere—nor did she find any broken glass on the floor of the lantern room or anywhere else in or near the tower. She took that to mean that while George may have enjoyed the drink, he didn't think the lighthouse was the place to be drinking.

Lorraine knows of at least one time when George seemed to be up to his old pranks at the light station. Fairly late one night, five young waitresses from a restaurant George and Lorraine had frequented came to visit Lorraine and find out more about the spirit light. They were paid that night and had carefully locked their purses inside one of the girl's cars before walking up the path from the parking lot to the keeper's dwelling.

After talking with Lorraine for a while, two of the girls decided to climb up to the lantern room to see for themselves what was making the light. Lorraine unlocked the tower door and waited at the bottom of the stairs for them. The first girl got about halfway up the staircase before turning around and hurrying back down saying that she had felt somebody other than her girlfriend inside the tower and didn't want to find out who it was. The other girl climbed all the way to the top, and when she came back down, she also reported feeling someone else in the tower, but she had just told whoever it was to leave her alone!

Lorraine relocked the tower door, and the girls said goodnight and walked back to the parking area. When they reached the car they had been so careful to lock, they found the doors unlocked. And when the driver started the engine everything in the car came on—the lights, the radio, and the horn!

If Lorraine is on duty when you visit Old Presque Isle Lighthouse, she will be glad to tell you more about George and the spirit light. She will also be glad to tell you the history of the light station and answer any questions you might have about the keeper's dwelling and the artifacts on display. She will even show you the exact spot in the backyard where she would have been struck by lightning if her protector hadn't prevented her from stepping out the back door of the dwelling that stormy September day in 1992.

Be sure to climb up to the top of the tower to see the empty electrical socket inside the Fresnel lens that can't rotate anymore. As you place your foot on the bottom rung of the short ladder up to the lantern room, call hello to George and tell him you just want to see the lens and the view. And before you start back down the ladder, be sure to tell him to keep up the good work of helping mariners find their way safely into Presque Isle Harbor.

When you visit Old Presque Isle Lighthouse, plan to have dinner at one of the local restaurants and linger until after dark, so you can see the spirit light for yourself. Leave your car in the marina parking lot

When you visit New Presque Isle Light Station, stand next to the tower and listen closely. You may hear a woman screaming—or perhaps it's just the fierce Lake Huron wind screaming around the lighthouse.

and walk out along the pier keeping your eye on the lighthouse.

About halfway out you will see the light come on, and it will blink on and off as you walk farther out on the pier. If you count the posts as you walk along the pier, you will find that you can see the light best at the thirty-seventh and thirty-ninth posts. You can also see the spirit light blink on and off as you drive along Grand Lake Road near the marina and if you go boating on the lake at night.

Before you leave the area, you may want to drive a mile farther up the peninsula and visit New Presque Isle Light Station. Completed in 1870, this taller tower went into active service at the beginning of the 1871 shipping season. The U.S. Coast Guard continues to maintain New Presque Isle Light Station as an active guide to navigation and opens the tower for tours from May 15 through October 15.

This new light station also seems to have a resident spirit, a woman who may have been the wife of one of the keepers. One version of her story says that the isolation and numbing routine of living on a light station drove her insane. Another version says that her husband locked her in the tower whenever he went to visit another woman in a nearby town. One way or another, the woman evidently died at the light station, and people have reported hearing her screaming—or perhaps it's just the fierce Lake Huron wind screaming around the tower. You may want to stand near the tower and listen for yourself.

Both Old and New Presque Isle Lighthouses are on Presque Isle peninsula north of Alpena, Michigan. Take Grand Lake Road north from the town of Presque Isle, go through the intersection with County Road 638, and continue toward the end of the peninsula. You will reach Old Presque Isle Lighthouse first; New Presque Isle Lighthouse is about a mile farther north on Grand Lake Road.

The tower and maritime museum at Old Presque Isle Lighthouse are open to the public from mid-May through mid-October; for more information, call 989/595-6979. The still-active tower at New Presque Isle Lighthouse is open to the public from mid-May through mid-October, and a maritime museum is located in the restored 1905 keeper's dwelling; for more information, call 989/595-9917.

You can also see the Old and New Presque Isle Lighthouses and others in the area by taking tours with Middle Island Light Station Tours. Call 989/619-1013 for reservations.

When Hannah Thomas's husband left his post at the light station on Gurnet Point to fight in the Revolutionary War, Hannah took over his responsibilities as keeper. When you visit Gurnet Point, you may see Hannah—apparently, she is still watching for his return home.

A Vigilant Widow Keeps Watch

Plymouth Lighthouse on Gurnet Point near Plymouth, Massachusetts

When most people their age were packing up their offices and looking forward to retirement, Bob and Sandra Shanklin started packing up their camera gear and looking for lighthouses to photograph. It all started when they took a trip to New England and visited a lighthouse. As Bob puts it, "Lighthouses are a virus with no known cure ... and the bug bit both of us."

The Shanklins now go on trips and photograph as many lighthouses as they can before "the money runs out." Then they return home to Fort Walton Beach, Florida, and sell their photographs until they have enough money to take another trip. They "barely survive," notes Sandra, but they have more fun than anyone she knows.

Bob and Sandra's goal became to photograph every lighthouse still standing in the United States, some 670 of them according to their count at the time. After they had photographed about 200 of the historic structures, the Associated Press caught up with them and did a

feature story about their quest. The story ran in newspapers nationwide, and people started calling the Shanklins
"The Lighthouse People,"a name that suits them well.

Bob and Sandra have shared many out-of-the-ordinary experiences on their way to light stations up and
down America's ocean, lake, and river shorelines.
Carrying heavy camera bags, they have trudged
through sand dunes in hundred-degree heat, waded
along trails flooded with knee-deep water, climbed up
rocks and out on limbs—all to capture our nation's
lighthouses on film before some of them disappear forever. The Lighthouse People have ridden over the
waves in more ferries, crabbers' boats, lobstermen's
boats, watermen's boats, shrimpers' boats, power-
boats, and rowboats than they can begin to count. And
they have flown in single-engine, twin-engine, and
seaplanes through conditions their pilots have told
them was the worst weather they'd ever seen.

One of their hair-raising experiences, however, was
head and shoulders more out-of-the-ordinary than any
of the others. It happened at Plymouth Lighthouse on
Gurnet Point, a spit of land that reaches out into the
Atlantic northeast of Plymouth, Massachusetts.

A lighthouse has stood on Gurnet Point since colonial
days, perhaps as early as the 1740s, to mark the northern
corner of the mouth of Plymouth Bay. In the late 1760s,
the Thomas family, who owned the property at the time,
agreed to allow lighthouse officials to build a dwelling
with two attached towers on their land if the Thomases
were awarded the job of keepers. The keeper's pay,
although relatively low, provided welcome extra income.

The twin lights of Gurnet Lighthouse officially began
service in 1769, and Keeper John Thomas faithfully kept

the oil lamp in each tower burning until he left to fight alongside his fellow colonists in the Revolutionary War. John's wife, Hannah, filled in for him as keeper while he was gone.

To help stop British vessels from entering Plymouth Bay during the war, the townspeople of Plymouth, Duxbury, and Kingston erected a fort near Gurnet Lighthouse. Colonists defending the fort exchanged cannon fire with the British frigate *Niger* when the vessel ran aground nearby, and one of the frigate's shots hit one of the lighthouse towers as Hannah stood watch.

Fortunately, that was the only damage Gurnet Lighthouse suffered during the war. Unfortunately, Hannah suffered the loss of her husband; he did not return at the end of the war and was presumed dead. Like a responsible keeper, Hannah continued to faithfully tend the lamps in the twin towers on Gurnet Point. In 1790 lighthouse officials awarded the keeper's post to Hannah, making her America's first female keeper.

The lighthouse on Gurnet Point has changed significantly from the days when Hannah lived in the keeper's dwelling and dutifully climbed up and down the steps inside the twin towers. The 1769 structure burned in 1801. It was replaced in 1803 by a new dwelling with taller twin towers spaced farther apart. Both towers, which were rebuilt in 1843, served as active navigational aids until 1924 when lighthouse officials decided it was not necessary to have two lights at the station. They decommissioned the northeast tower, removed the fourth-order Fresnel lens, and dismantled the structure. The south tower, which became known as Plymouth Lighthouse, now houses a solar-powered optic and continues to flash its distinctive white and red beams.

Despite all these changes—and the fact that Plymouth Lighthouse no longer needs a resident keeper—Hannah may still be keeping watch at her lighthouse.

When Bob and Sandra went to photograph this historic light station, they decided to spend the night in the old keeper's dwelling. The only other person officially on the light station grounds with them at the time was a U.S. Coast Guardsman who was making some repairs.

When the Shanklins went to bed that night, they could see the red and white beams from the lighthouse through the window of the room where they were sleeping. Sandra says it was like having a sign go on and off, making the room alternately light and dark.

Despite the flashing light, they had no trouble falling asleep, but something woke Bob in the middle of the night. He remembers raising up on his elbow and watching the revolving light go around once or twice. After he had been awake a minute or two, he turned to look at Sandra, who was still sleeping soundly beside him. That's when he saw her.

"I saw a woman's face hovering about fifteen or sixteen inches above Sandra's face," says Bob. "She had a blue-green, iridescent appearance, and she was wearing an old-timey garment that buttoned tight around her long neck.

"Her long dark hair was neatly parted and flowed down to her shoulders," he adds. "Her complexion was smooth, but her cheeks were very sunken. She didn't have any wrinkles or gray hair. I guessed she might be in her mid-thirties.

"What I remember most," continues Bob, "is her sad eyes. They were the saddest eyes I have ever seen."

Bob notes that he didn't feel frightened or threatened in any way by the woman—he was just surprised at seeing her. And he felt her intense sadness. "As I continued to look at her, I noticed that the corners of her mouth twitched once or twice as if she might be trying to say something," says Bob. "I've been kicking myself ever since that I didn't speak to her."

As Bob looked into the woman's face, he was aware that the revolving lighthouse beacon brightened the room several times. He turned away from the woman to look at the light, and when he turned back, she had vanished. "I hate that I didn't wake up Sandra, so she could see her, too," says Bob. "And I hate that I waited until morning to say anything about seeing her."

When Bob did tell Sandra about the sad young woman he had seen the night before, they began to speculate about who she might be. They asked the coast guardsman who was staying at the light station if he had seen the woman or if he knew of any ghosts that had been reported earlier, but he didn't. They asked several other people, but no one knew of any ghostly appearances at the light station.

Given the woman's old-fashioned attire and the fact that she had appeared in the master bedroom of the dwelling, Bob and Sandra surmised that she was prob ably one of the keepers' wives who had lived at the light station in the late eighteenth or nineteenth century. Bob has a white beard and looks quite a bit like an old-time lighthouse keeper. Perhaps the sad young woman was Hannah Thomas, and she thought Bob was her missing husband, John, finally returning home to the keeper's dwelling after fighting in the Revolutionary War. Perhaps Hannah had come to find out who the woman was with the man who looked like her long-lost husband.

Or perhaps the young woman was the wife of another keeper who had lost his life at the station, or perhaps a ship captain's wife whose husband had not returned safely to port. Or perhaps she was the surviving half of a shipwrecked couple. Over the centuries many young women have endured the sadness and pain of losing a loved one to the ocean off this lonely stretch of North Atlantic coastline.

Bob and Sandra still puzzle over their extraordinary experience at historic Plymouth Lighthouse, and they still continue to have out-of-the-ordinary experiences on their lighthouse travels. Many times when they head out on the morning of a shoot, fog or stormy weather threatens to ruin their photo opportunity. But just as they arrive at the lighthouse du jour, the clouds part and the sun comes out. They have experienced this serendipitous turn of events so often that Bob says "it means they are doing what they were meant to do."

Even after capturing all of America's lighthouses on film, the Shanklins probably won't ever stop photographing these historic structures. "We can always go back for a better photo," explains Sandra. "On our trips we are at the mercy of the weather and through no fault of our own often are not able to get that beautiful photo we hoped for."

You may want to travel to Massachusetts to see historic Plymouth Lighthouse for yourself. Just standing on the shore of the Atlantic at Gurnet Point will take you back in time. "Many things happened near [Gurnet Lighthouse] before and after it was built," says Sandra. "They say the Vikings landed here. There is an American Indian burial ground. And so close to Plymouth, who's to say how many Pilgrims came here as well as sailors and sea captains?"

Perhaps you too will encounter the young woman with the saddest eyes you'll ever see. If you do, please ask her why she is so sad—and be sure to let Bob Shanklin know what she says.

Plymouth Lighthouse stands at Gurnet Point at the northeastern entrance to Plymouth Bay. Please respect the privacy of the residents who live near the light station when you travel along this stretch of the Massachusetts coastline.

The motherly ghost known as "Rue" haunts Heceta Head Lighthouse as she mourns for her lost home and child. In 1996 she was joined by a ghost named "John" who followed Carol and Mike Korgan—or maybe just their couch—to Heceta Head.

A "Neat Old Lady" and a "Neat Old Man" Take Care of the Keepers

Heceta Head Lighthouse near Florence, Oregon

When caretakers Carol and Mike Korgan moved into the restored assistant keeper's dwelling at Heceta Head Lighthouse in the spring of 1996, they already knew about the lady ghost who lived there. What they didn't know was that they brought a gentleman ghost with them. But what better place for a lady and a gentleman to meet than Heceta Head, one of the most picturesque and romantic lighthouses on the West Coast!

Almost all lighthouses evoke a sense of the romantic, but a dash of royal intrigue enhances the aura of
bravery, adventure, danger, and heroism at Heceta
Head. This lighthouse bears the name of Portuguese
explorer Don Bruno de Heceta, a daring New World
seafarer who discovered this remote headland while
he was on a secret mission for the royal family of
Spain. Heceta set sail from San Blas, Mexico, aboard a
Spanish Royal Navy vessel in early 1775. His top secret
orders were to travel up the Pacific Coast all the way
to the Arctic Circle, going ashore frequently along the
coastline to erect crosses and claim the land for Spain.
Heceta made it as far north as the mouth of the
Columbia River before turning back to seek help for
his scurvy-stricken crewmen.

When Heceta sailed past what later became known
as Heceta Head, he recorded that the water appeared
shallow quite some distance from shore. As nineteenth-

For as far back as anyone can remember, a woman in an old-fashioned dress has been taking care of things at the keeper's dwellings at Heceta Head Lighthouse. You may see her watching you from the attic window, or you may find her keeping company with her new friend, "John."

century mariners sometimes found out the hard way, the waters off this rugged headland indeed are shallow, just as the explorer had suspected. And as seaports sprang up along the West Coast and shipping traffic and shipwrecks increased, the need for a lighthouse at Heceta Head grew.

In the late 1880s, members of the U.S. Congress approved $80,000 for a light station to be built at the headland, but mariners had to continue navigating the dangerous coastline on their own for more than five years. It took workmen that long to build wagon roads to the cliff-top construction site, secure the needed building materials, and complete the tower, the spacious head keeper's dwelling, the two-family assistant keepers' dwelling, the oil-storage buildings, and other outbuildings.

Heceta Head's newly appointed head keeper lit the five-wick lamp inside the first-order lens for the first time at the end of March 1894. For some reason neither the head keeper nor his two assistants stayed very long in the early days at Heceta Head, and the official records don't tell us much about these men or their families. But the grave of a baby girl on the light station grounds indicates that, like parents everywhere, one of these late-nineteenth-century keepers and his wife suffered the wrenching sadness of having a child die in infancy.

The lady ghost who has lived in the assistant keepers' duplex for as far back as people can remember may be the mother of the baby girl buried at Heceta Head. Carol and Mike call her Rue, a name that popped up years ago when someone used a Ouija board to find out the ghost's identity. Mike describes Rue as a "neat old lady," a "motherly" type. He says that she doesn't go out of her way to cause problems, but she does seem to be very concerned about things being done to the house.

Once, for instance, Rue evidently was not happy with the work being done by a group of volunteers who were helping with a painting project. The work crew spent the night in the keepers' dwelling, and in the wee hours of the morning, the fire alarm went off for no apparent reason. And it kept going off for no apparent reason. Once the weary workers were convinced there was no danger of fire anywhere in the building, they removed the battery from the alarm—but it still kept going off!

In the past Rue has reportedly removed a box of rat poison and replaced it with an old-fashioned stocking. She also has been credited with opening cupboard doors and moving objects from one place to another. Rue seems to make her presence known whenever changes or repairs are being made at her dwelling.

Perhaps, though, Rue and her husband and their baby girl didn't originally live in the two-family dwelling that still stands at the light station. Perhaps her husband was the head keeper, and they lived in the larger, single-family dwelling that the U.S. Coast Guard, for undocumented reasons, razed in 1940. Electrifying the lamp in the tower in the mid-1930s had decreased the amount of work—and consequently the number of keepers—needed to maintain the light and buildings at Heceta Head. With only two keepers assigned to the station, officials housed the head keeper and his assistant as well as their families in the duplex. Perhaps Rue had been forced to move out of the larger dwelling and is mourning the loss of her home as well as the loss of her little girl. Perhaps she is fearful that the smaller dwelling will also be razed, and she will have no home left near her baby's grave. Perhaps that is why Rue becomes restless whenever people start doing things to the existing dwelling.

Keepers continued to live in Rue's dwelling until the U.S. Coast Guard automated the light in July 1963. Although coast guardsmen continued to maintain the tower and light after that time, they abandoned the two-family dwelling. The U.S. Forest Service eventually obtained ownership of the abandoned property and rented the dwelling to employees of nearby Siuslaw National Forest. By 1970 the dwelling had fallen into serious disrepair and seemed headed for demolition when Don Bowman, of the Siuslaw Museum Association, formed the Friends of Heceta House to help guide future use of the property. Within a short time Lane Community College officials obtained a lease to use the dwelling and grounds for educational purposes with the long-term goal of preserving the buildings at the historic light station.

One of the best things to come out of this arrangement with the college was the repairwork done on the keepers' dwelling. Rue, however, may have been agitated by the increased activity in her house. One day when a handyman was working in the attic, he noticed someone's reflection in one of the windows. He turned around to see who had come up so quietly behind him and came face to face with Rue. He noticed that she was wearing a long, old-fashioned dress, had silver-gray hair, and was looking at him pleadingly—as if she were asking him to help her. Rue startled the handyman so much that he didn't stay in the attic long enough to ask her who she was or what she wanted him to do for her—he just took off down the stairs and refused to go back up.

Later when the man was working on the exterior of the house, he accidentally broke one of the attic windows. He replaced the broken pane from the outside but refused to go back inside to sweep up the shattered glass in the attic. The caretakers reported hearing scraping noises coming from the attic that night. The next day when they went upstairs to see if they could figure out what had made the noises, they found that someone had swept the pieces of the broken glass into a neat pile under the repaired window.

Rue may have been pleased when Heceta Head Light Station was placed on the National Register of Historic Places in 1978 because that ensures the preservation of her dwelling as well as the other buildings and grounds. The exterior of the two-family keepers' dwelling has now been restored to its original 1890s appearance. Inside, one side of the duplex is being restored to its original 1890s appearance and the other to its pre-U.S. Coast Guard 1930s appearance.

Over the years, workmen, caretakers, and college students using the dwelling as a classroom or overnight retreat have reported finding missing or moved objects, hearing dainty footsteps in the attic, seeing an elderly woman looking down at them from an attic window, and catching glimpses of a smoky female figure they nicknamed the "Gray Lady." Mike and Carol haven't actually seen Rue yet, but they know she's in the dwelling because they can smell her floral perfume.

One morning, not long ago, when they didn't have bed-and-breakfast guests to feed, Carol and Mike decided to enjoy a leisurely breakfast. Just as they were sitting down to eat, the telephone rang. Mike got up from the table to answer the phone, Carol got up to take the toast out of the toaster, and they both got back to the table at the same time. Mike noticed that milk had been poured over the oatmeal in his bowl and immediately chided Carol for doing it—he reminded her that they had been married for thirty-eight years, and she knew he didn't like milk on his oatmeal. Carol replied that she had not poured the milk on his oatmeal.

That's when they realized that Rue had done it, and a few days later they found out what might have prompted her action. Lab tests done as part of Mike's annual checkup showed that his calcium level was low. Perhaps in her motherly way Rue was encouraging Mike to put milk on his oatmeal, so he would get the calcium she knew he needed!

Unlike Rue, John, the gentleman ghost, had never lived at Heceta Head Light Station before the spring of 1996. He just tagged along with Carol and Mike when they left their house in Portland and moved into the keepers' dwelling. The couple had experienced some unexplained, prankish goings-on in their Portland house—a wonderful, huge place with secret passageways and servants' quarters on the third floor. When they asked the previous owner, John's son, if he knew about any ghosts in the house, he told them the ghost was his father. John had committed suicide in the house during the Depression, and evidently his spirit had never left—until Carol and Mike moved out.

It turns out that John is attached to a particular antique couch that had been in the Portland house when Carol and Mike bought it. Not knowing about the connection, the couple had tried to sell—and even give away—that piece of old furniture before they moved to Heceta Head. But everyone who took the couch invariably brought it back for one reason or another. Finally Carol and Mike gave in and decided to take the couch with them to their new home. When they started experiencing the same unexplained pranks in the keepers' dwelling, they realized that it wasn't the Portland house that was haunted—it was the antique couch!

Mike describes John as a "neat old guy" who has given him good advice over the years. If Mike is restless or wakes up in the middle of the night, all he has to do is sit on the old couch and talk with John—and he feels better. Some of the bed-and-breakfast guests who have stayed in the keepers' dwelling at Heceta Head have reported sitting on the couch and feeling so much at peace that they have fallen sound asleep.

John seems to have made himself pretty much at home in the keepers' dwelling at Heceta Head, and Carol and Mike hope that he and Rue have become friends. The romantic lighthouse setting, plus Carol's and Mike's training as chefs and their years of experience as restaurant owners, has made Heceta Head a popular site for wedding celebrations. Perhaps someday Carol and Mike will cater Rue and John's wedding reception—or perhaps they already have and just didn't see the happy couple and their guests!

Carol and Mike Korgan—and Rue and John—would be delighted to have you visit them at lovely Heceta Head Light Station. You can tour the beautifully restored buildings, climb the tower, and hear entertaining stories that span more than a century of lighthouse history. You can spend the night at the keepers' dwelling in one of three second-floor bedrooms: the Mariner's Room, the Lighthouse Room, and the Victorian Room. Even if you don't spend the night, be sure to go upstairs and sit a spell on the couch with John—you'll find it in the hallway outside the bedrooms. You may even want to venture up to the attic to meet Rue—or you may find her keeping company with John on the antique couch on the second floor.

As part of your overnight stay, you will enjoy one of Carol and Mike's delicious breakfasts. You may even decide to ask these American Culinary Foundation-certified chefs to cater a special event for you at Heceta Head.

Heceta Head Light Station is about 12 miles north of Florence, Oregon. Take U.S. 101 north along the coast from Florence and follow the signs to the lighthouse.

For more information about when the buildings are open for tours and to make reservations to spend the night or for special events, contact Heceta Head Lighthouse, 92072 Highway 101 South, Yachats, OR 97498; 866/547-3696. Or visit www.HecetaLighthouse.com.

Head Keeper William Prior demanded that things be done right. When you spend the night at Big Bay Point Light Station, which is open as a bed and breakfast year-round, you may find him turning off the shower if he thinks you are wasting water.

Head Keeper William Prior Still Wants Things Done His Way

Big Bay Point Lighthouse on Lake Superior near Big Bay, Michigan

L ighthouse keepers tended to be very responsible employees. They had to be or they would lose their jobs!

Lighthouse officials had at least one rule and/or regulation for *everything* at a light station, from the ventilator ball on the roof of the tower to the dust under the beds in the keeper's dwelling. And lighthouse inspectors made both scheduled and unscheduled visits to make sure the keepers and their families were following *all* the rules and regulations *all* the time. During their white-glove inspections, lighthouse inspectors duly noted every instance of noncompliance, from a smudge on a miniscule piece of brass to a speck of dirt on the kitchen floor.

If a keeper wanted to remain a keeper, he or she had to make sure that every item at the station was always clean and in its proper place, and that all procedures were followed to the letter. Those stringent requirements suited William Prior just fine.

William served as the first head keeper at Big Bay Point Lighthouse, which began active service in 1896. Official lighthouse records and the notes William wrote in his logbook indicate that he was a perfectionist who demanded perfection from his assistant keeper. Understandably, William had a hard time finding and keeping an assistant. After a number of assistants had failed to meet William's standards and had either quit or been fired, William arranged for his son to get the job.

Unfortunately, William's son accidentally cut himself while working at the light station in April 1901. The cut became infected, but William waited until June to take him the thirty miles to Marquette for medical treatment. By that time gangrene had set in, and the young man soon died.

Continuing to perform like a top-notch, responsible employee, William returned to his post at Big Bay Point Lighthouse immediately after his son's funeral. But William's grief over the loss of his son—perhaps along with some guilt about waiting too long to take him to the doctor—proved to be stronger than his sense of job responsibility. The day after William returned to the light station, he disappeared.

Search parties scoured the forest bordering the lighthouse grounds, and a reward was posted for information on the whereabouts of William Prior, but all to no immediate avail. It wasn't until the end of September, some three months later, that a man walking through the woods about a mile from the lighthouse happened upon William's body. Evidently he had committed suicide.

But Head Keeper William Prior's spirit may have continued to live on at Big Bay Point Lighthouse after his untimely death. Perhaps this obsessively responsible employee was—and still is—trying to make amends for shirking his responsibilities and abandoning his post. John Gale, Linda Gamble, and Jeff Gamble, Big Bay Point's current owners, haven't actually seen William in the keeper's dwelling or on the grounds as have some former owners and bed-and-breakfast guests. But they know William is there because he sometimes makes—or at least tries to make—things happen *his* way, the *right* way according to the old rules and regulations.

For instance, if someone turns on the shower and then steps out of the room, William turns off the water. Perhaps he does it to remind guests of the old adage "waste not, want not." And sometimes William shuts off lights—again perhaps to conserve resources, something keepers and their families had to do to survive. William and every other lighthouse keeper knew how to stretch meager government-issued supplies and how to make do or do without. Keepers had to be frugal, and head keepers even more so since they were ultimately responsible for the well-being of everyone at their light station as well as the well-being of the mariners who depended on the lighthouse for safe passage along the coast. Head Keeper William Prior may just be trying to keep Big Bay Point Lighthouse running at peak efficiency.

William also opens and closes cupboard doors—perhaps just checking to make sure everything is clean and in its place in case the lighthouse inspector pops in for a surprise visit and runs his white-gloved hand over a shelf or two. One winter night when Linda was manning the light station by herself, some of the bed-and-breakfast guests stayed out late enough to close the local bar in nearby Big Bay. Sometime around 2 a.m., after Linda had secured the door behind the last incoming guest and climbed into bed, she heard cupboard doors opening and closing. At first she thought it was one of the guests looking for a glass to get a drink of water, but the opening and closing noises kept going on and on.

Finally Linda got up and went to the kitchen to investigate, but nobody was there. Exasperated and tired, Linda said as firmly as she could, "Okay, Will. I know ghosts don't like people moving things, and we have been doing that, but we're really trying to make things the way they used to be. I have to get up early and make breakfast for these folks, Will, so cut it out!"

William evidently did what Linda told him to do because the noises stopped—at least for the rest of that night.

While William's ghost makes his presence known in the part of the dwelling where he lived as head keeper as well as on the light station grounds, bed-and-breakfast guests have reported seeing the ghost of a young woman on the second floor of the assistant keeper's quarters. Guests say she appears to be a modern-day girl in her late teens.

Jeff says they did extensive research to find out whether a teenage girl had died at the lighthouse within the last fifty years or so, and they also checked available missing person's reports for the Big Bay Point area. They had a hard time finding public records for the 1950s because once the U.S. Coast

Guard automated the light and abandoned the property in the early 1940s, the nearby town of Big Bay nearly became a ghost town. They found no official records of a young woman living or dying at Big Bay Point Lighthouse, but they did learn the unpublished details of an accident at the lighthouse from a family in the area.

John, Jeff, and Linda believe the young female ghost is probably Sarah, a teenager who went to the abandoned light station with some of her friends a number of years ago. The teenagers were goofing around when Sarah fell and broke her neck. Frightened, the others just left her body where she had fallen. Some time passed before her family learned about Sarah's death.

The current owners downplay the presence of Will and Sarah at Big Bay Point because they don't want people to come to the light station expecting to have a supernatural experience. They want people to come to experience firsthand something of what it was like to live and work at the historic lighthouse. Jeff, Linda, and John invite people to leave the modern-day world behind and step back in time to the early 1900s when keepers and their families lived there.

The existing two-story brick structure with its 60-foot-tall square tower was completed in 1896. Originally, it was a duplex that housed the head keeper, his assistant, and their families. Each half of the duplex had a kitchen, dining room, and parlor on the first floor and three bedrooms upstairs. The attached five-story tower had a combination keeper's office/schoolroom on the first floor, a combination chart-map room/chapel on the second, and storage areas on the third. The top two floors held the lantern room, lens, and the clockwork machinery to turn the lens.

Keepers continued to maintain the light inside Big Bay Point's third-order Fresnel lens until 1941 when the U.S. Coast Guard placed an automated beacon atop a steel tower on the grounds and darkened the original tower. Over the next two decades, the abandoned building fell into serious disrepair. In the early 1960s Chicago surgeon Dr. John Pick purchased the dwelling and surrounding grounds. He remodeled the interior of the historic structure and used it as his summer residence for almost twenty years.

In the late 1970s Dan Hitchens, a Michigan business executive, bought the property and installed some additional modern conveniences. For the next five years, Dan invited harried businessmen to use the comfortable, peaceful dwelling as a retreat.

Norman "Buck" Gotschall and his two business partners bought Big Bay Point in 1985 and opened it to the public as a bed-and-breakfast the following year. Buck persistently petitioned the U.S. Coast Guard to relight the historic tower, and in 1990 they granted his request. About this time John, Jeff, and Linda began visiting Big Bay Point as a getaway from their work on a restoration project at the Frank Lloyd Wright Home and Studio in Oak Park, Illinois. They bought the historic light station in 1992 and have continued to restore the dwelling and tower.

These avid preservationists are concerned about the hundreds of historic lighthouses that have been abandoned, destroyed by vandals, or lost forever to fire or storms. By continuing to restore Big Bay Point Lighthouse and encouraging people to spend a night in this historic structure, they believe they are helping secure the survival of this lighthouse for generations to come.

They dedicate part of the room rate paid by their bed-and-breakfast guests to ongoing preservation and restoration projects at the light station.

John, Jeff, and Linda invite you to visit this lovely old lighthouse and to experience for yourself a little bit of what it was like to live along this scenic stretch of Lake Superior shoreline in the early part of the twentieth century. You can visit the light station grounds and stay overnight in the lighthouse year-round (the roads are kept clear in winter). You can also take guided tours of the light station from May through September.

If you should happen to see Head Keeper William Prior or Sarah when you visit Big Bay Point Lighthouse, please let John, Jeff, and Linda know. And if William keeps turning off the shower or shutting off the lights in your room, just politely tell him to cut it out!

Big Bay Point Lighthouse is about 30 miles north of Marquette. Take County Road 550 north to Big Bay and then follow the signs to the lighthouse and inn.

For more information about touring the grounds and to make overnight reservations, contact Big Bay Point Lighthouse, #3 Lighthouse Road, Big Bay, MI 49808; 906/345-9957; or visit www.BigBayLighthouse.com.

Members of the St. Augustine Junior Service League have beautifully restored this light station, making it one of the best places to experience firsthand what it was like to be a lighthouse keeper. You may also experience firsthand a number of friendly spirits who are doing their part to bring the past to life at this historic site.

A Young Girl, a Cigar Smoker, a Tall Older Man, and Albert Make Their Presence Known

St. Augustine Lighthouse
in St. Augustine, Florida

A bout 10:30 p.m. one Friday in September 1998, Public Relations Coordinator Celeste Halsema took her out-of-town guest, Debra, to St. Augustine Lighthouse to show her how lovely the lighthouse looks at night. As they walked across the lawn between the tower and keepers' dwelling, Celeste told Debra about an incident some months earlier when she and four men from a PBS film crew were in the oil-storage building at the base of the tower. Celeste said

she suddenly smelled very strong, fresh cigar smoke
and asked the crewmen if they smelled it too. They did,
and one of the men promptly announced: "Okay, it's
time—let's leave!"

Celeste told Debra it was not the first ghost she
and other people had encountered at the light station.
Debra asked about the other ghosts, and Celeste started telling her about the young girl who seems to live
in the keepers' dwelling. Debra suddenly grabbed
Celeste's arm and asked if the girl had dark hair. When
Celeste said yes, Debra responded, "We've got to
leave—right now!"

When Celeste asked why they had to leave, Debra
said she would explain later and then bolted for the
car. Celeste hurried after Debra, who was running—not
walking—as fast as she could. By the time Celeste
reached the driver's door, Debra was already inside the
car with the door locked on her side. Once they were
out of the parking lot and on the way to Celeste's
house, Debra explained that while they were standing
on the lawn talking she had seen something move in
one of the upstairs windows of the keepers' dwelling.
When she took a second look, she saw a girl wearing a
red dress. Their eyes had caught and held for a second
or two, and then the girl had flipped her long dark hair
back over her shoulders and disappeared—not disappeared as in walked away from the window but disappeared as in *vanished.* Debra said she didn't feel threatened by the girl in any way—she was just so unnerved
to see *her* that she needed to get away from there.

Celeste knew Debra was not making up the story
because she had seen the goose bumps on Debra's
arms. Celeste also knew the light station had closed to

the public more than four hours earlier, so there was
virtually no chance that a female visitor was upstairs in
the dwelling at 10:30 p.m.

Celeste specifically questioned Debra about the
color of the girl's dress, whether it was a shade of rose,
like the drapes that hung down the sides of the window. Debra said no, the girl's dress was darker than
the drapes—the girl was wearing a *red* dress. And
Debra pointedly added, "Our eyes caught—she looked
straight at me!"

The next day when Celeste was back at the light
station, she made a point of going upstairs in the
dwelling to see if the lights on the porch could have
backlit an object that might appear to be the figure of a
girl standing in the window. But she could find nothing
that would create such an illusion. Nor did she find any
furniture or anything else out of place in the room
where her friend had seen the girl. Celeste also double-
checked the color of the drapes. They were indeed
rose—not red, and the backing was white. So there
was no way the drapes could appear to be any color
darker than rose.

Some people think the girl in the keepers' dwelling is
the ghost of a child who died in an accident on July 10,
1873, when the existing tower was under construction.
According to documents and photographs in the St.
Augustine Lighthouse and Museum archives, the lighthouse construction superintendent, his wife, and their
five children lived at the site while the tower was being
built. On that fateful day in July, the superintendent's fif-
teen- and thirteen-year-old girls were playing with
another girl, as they often did, in a tram that was used
to carry supplies up a railway from the dock on shore to

the construction site. The tram suddenly broke loose, hurtled down the rails, and dumped the three girls into the water. All of them drowned.

Other people say the girl in the keepers' dwelling can't be one of the three girls who drowned that day because the ghost is too young. Besides, the existing keepers' dwelling wasn't completed until 1876, two years after the accident. Although her identity remains somewhat of a mystery, this dark-haired young girl, who often wears a big bow in her hair, definitely makes her presence known at St. Augustine Lighthouse and Museum.

After the U.S. Coast Guard automated the light in the tower at St. Augustine in 1955, which eliminated the need for a resident keeper, the dwelling was rented to private citizens. Several people who slept in one of the upstairs bedrooms during this time reported being awakened during the night by a young girl in old-fashioned dress. Just as she had done with Celeste's friend Debra, the young girl got the attention of the nighttime guests, caught eyes with them, and then vanished.

A suspicious fire in 1970 gutted the hundred-year-old keepers' dwelling, which by that time had been declared surplus government property and been allowed to fall into disrepair. In 1980 the Junior Service League of St. Augustine undertook the massive project of restoring the dwelling as well as the tower, which also had suffered from neglect.

A woman who lives in St. Augustine has visited the restored light station several times in recent years, says Celeste, but she always declines to go inside the keepers' dwelling. The woman feels there is something "very sad" in the house.

Well, the young girl may be sad, but she still seems to enjoy playing pranks on unsuspecting visitors. Occasionally, a group will rent a large upstairs room in the dwelling for a meeting, wedding reception, or other special event. This particular room has four entrances, each with a door that can be locked. Sometimes when people try to leave the room, they discover that someone has locked the doors, and sometimes someone keeps locking and unlocking the doors—the kind of thing a bored youngster might do to keep herself amused.

The young girl is not the only unofficial resident living in the keepers' dwelling. Over the years, quite a number of staff members and visitors have encountered a tall older man in the basement. Executive Director Kathy Fleming was in the basement hallway one day when she caught a glimpse of *him* in one of the storage rooms. Some of the Junior Service League volunteers and Cullen Chambers, a lighthouse historian who worked on the restoration of the tower from 1990 to 1994, have felt cold spots in the basement and sensed an unseen presence. Kathy, Cullen, and the others who have seen or felt the presence didn't sense that it was going to harm them in any way. Like Celeste's friend Debra and the PBS camera crew, they were just startled to encounter an unexplained someone. Perhaps the tall older man is one of the keepers from many years ago who for one reason or another simply refuses to give up his post.

Recently, one of the light station employees had a more interactive encounter with the man in the basement. The employee was rearranging the benches in the small theater where visitors view a film about St.

Augustine Lighthouse. He picked up one end of a long bench and moved it back, and just as he set down that end of the bench, someone picked up the other end and set it down right where it was supposed to go! Wide-eyed, the employee flew upstairs to tell the other staff members about his unseen helper. Having known the employee for quite some time, no one doubted that his story was true. Perhaps the tall older man in the basement was lending a helping hand—just as a good lighthouse keeper would

On the other hand, a ghost named Albert seems intent on playing less-than-helpful pranks on the staff of the gift shop in the keepers' dwelling. For a number of years, Albert has reportedly been moving things around, knocking items off shelves, and on one occasion blowing prints of St. Augustine Lighthouse off a display rack.

As for the cigar-smoking ghost Celeste and the PBS crew encountered in the oil-storage building at the base of the lighthouse, at least one other person also encountered him that same evening. A woman standing on the lawn between the tower and the keepers' dwelling independently reported smelling "very strong, fresh cigar smoke." And from time to time, the interpreters who give tours of the lighthouse have reported smelling cigar smoke. They also have reported hearing a person climbing the tower stairs—but the someone never appears at the top of the staircase.

When the light station closes to the public every night and the interpreters have made sure everyone has left the tower, they lock the doors at the top and bottom of the staircase and electronically secure them. Even so, staff members occasionally see someone— sometimes a man, sometimes a woman—up on the catwalk outside the lantern room after hours. And sometimes after the interpreters punch in the code for the bottom door and climb up the stairs, they find that someone has already opened the door at the top!

This has happened enough times, says Celeste, that it can't be attributed to the interpreter on duty at the end of the day simply forgetting to lock the door. Besides, clearing the tower at the end of the day and locking the doors is part of the interpreters' normal routine. But climbing the stairs and opening the tower doors is part of the normal routine for a lighthouse keeper too—so perhaps one of St. Augustine's old keepers is simply continuing on his daily rounds at the light station.

Perhaps the stair climber or the cigar smoker who frequents the tower is Joseph Andreu, a keeper who slipped off his homemade scaffolding and fell some 60 feet to his death when he was painting the outside of the original 1824 tower. After Joseph's death, light-house officials awarded the job of keeper to his widow—so perhaps Joseph and/or his wife are the figures people see out on the catwalk at night.

Joseph died in the late 1850s, almost twenty-five years before the existing 1874 tower replaced the old 1824 lighthouse, which beach erosion threatened to—and finally did—topple. The existing tower stands about a half mile from the site of the lighthouse Joseph gave his life to maintain. But perhaps he decided to stay on the job after his death and both he and his wife simply moved into the new tower when their light-house fell into the sea in 1880.

Although the waves and wind have assaulted the 1874 tower for almost 125 years now, it stands firm. A powerful earthquake reportedly swayed the tower for

40 seconds in 1879, but the well-built structure survived unscathed except for some cracks in the walls. St. Augustine Lighthouse continued to send out its life-saving beam until September 1991, when the U.S. Coast Guard darkened the tower and removed the lens, which had been seriously damaged in December 1986 when a young vandal focused a high-powered rifle at the lantern room and took two shots. The shots blasted a hole in the center of the first-order beehive-shaped Fresnel lens and shattered 19 of the 320 prisms. The Coast Guard allowed the lighthouse to continue active service for five years after the incident, until an inspection indicated that the vibrations from irregular rotations were further damaging the delicately balanced, handcrafted optic.

The Coast Guard wanted to install an airport beacon in the historic tower, but public outcry demanded

Thanks to the Junior Service League's Fight to Save the Light, St. Augustine Lighthouse was repaired and now serves as a fully functioning lighthouse, offering visitors a chance to experience what life as a lighthouse keeper was like.

that the Junior Service League first be given a chance to find someone—and the money—to make the costly repairs needed to restore the damaged lens. Individuals and organizations from around the world joined the Fight to Save the Light, and in less than two years the lens was repaired. On May 22, 1993, St. Augustine Lighthouse returned to active service with its original Fresnel lens back in its rightful place.

The Junior Service League's long-term commitment to

restore and preserve St. Augustine Lighthouse has made it one of the very best places in the world to experience firsthand what it was like to live and work at a lighthouse. When you visit, be sure to climb the 219 steps to the top to see the magnificent first-order Fresnel lens and spectacular panoramic view, and when it gets dark, look for the flashing white beam that reaches up to 25 nautical miles out to sea. Also allow plenty of time to view the video and exhibits in the keepers' dwelling, visit the gift shop, and admire the authentically landscaped grounds.

And if you catch a glimpse of a dark-haired young girl, smell fresh cigar smoke, have an unseen helper lend you a hand, or hear the staff talking about Albert's latest prank, don't be alarmed. These friendly spirits are just doing their part to bring the past to life at historic St. Augustine Lighthouse.

St. Augustine Lighthouse and Museum stands at 81 Lighthouse Avenue on Anastasia Island near downtown St. Augustine. To reach the island, take Florida Highway A1A toward St. Augustine Beach. You will see the red-roofed, black-and-white, spiral-striped lighthouse to your left as you cross the Bridge of the Lions. The light station is open to the public year-round.

For more information contact St. Augustine Lighthouse and Museum, 81 Lighthouse Avenue, St. Augustine, FL 32084; 904/829-0745.

To read firsthand stories from Wilma Daniels Thompson, Cardell "Cracker" Daniels, and Edward Hewett Shepherd, who lived at St. Augustine Lighthouse in the 1920s and 1930s, see *Lighthouse Families* by Cheryl Shelton-Roberts and Bruce Roberts (Crane Hill Publishers, 1997 and 2006).

High tide floods the walkway between the mainland and the lighthouse at Battery Point. But even when the caretakers are temporarily cut off from civilization, they are never completely alone—the "Misty Friends" who live in the house always keep them company.

The "Misty Friends" Keep the Caretakers Company

Battery Point Lighthouse in Crescent City, California

Nancy Schnider absolutely does not believe in ghosts. And she has not noticed any unusual occurrences at Battery Point Lighthouse—at least not yet.

Nadine Tugel didn't believe in ghosts either when she moved into the lighthouse, but she ended up writing a twelve-page booklet about the "Misty Friends" who kept her and her husband, Jerry, company while they lived there. In "Battery Point Lighthouse: History, Artifacts, and Keepers," Nadine says that she and Jerry had heard the stories about things moving from one place to another seemingly on their own, lost objects turning up in unexpected places, things breaking without explanation, and other disconcerting happenings.

But, says Nadine, "I'll be the first to admit that I took this all in with a big grain of salt—until the day I was working in the radio room and heard a crash in the living room."

Nadine was ready to "kill" her cats for knocking something over until she looked down and saw the two of them standing beside her looking as surprised as she was. She went to the living room to investigate and found the shattered pieces of a cranberry-colored glass chimney from an antique candleholder on the floor. No one was in the room. Nothing else was out of order. And the candleholder itself was still sitting firmly in its place.

Nadine cleaned up the broken glass that day and didn't think much more about the unexplained crash—until the day she was telling a tour group about the artifacts in the living room and noticed one of the women suddenly step aside as if to let someone pass by her. The woman was standing in the doorway that opened to the tower, which rises up through the center of the dwelling. As the woman told Nadine later, she was listening to Nadine talk when "she felt someone put their hand on her side like they wanted to pass her" as they came out of the tower. The woman had courteously stepped aside and then turned around to see who was passing—but no one was there. "I believe you have ghosts," the woman had told Nadine.

Nadine tucked that incident away in her mind and didn't think much more about it—until another woman who was standing in the tower doorway felt someone touch her from behind as if asking her to move out of the way. The woman courteously stepped aside and turned around to look—but saw no one.

The Tugels' cats probably acknowledged the presence of the lighthouse's unofficial residents long before Nadine and Jerry did. Frisbie, their tortoiseshell half-bobcat, seemed particularly sensitive to the Misty Friends. For the most part, Frisbie seemed to accept the unseen presences and even interacted with them from time to time. Quite often Nadine and other family members would find Frisbie sitting in the doorway between the living room and kitchen "batting her front paws like someone was dangling a ribbon or toy in front of her." At first they thought Frisbie was batting at a bug on the wall, but no matter how hard they looked, they never saw a bug or any other plaything that would interest the cat.

Like the two tourists who had stepped aside when someone was trying to pass by them at the base of the tower, Frisbie also stepped aside to let someone pass by her in the tower. Frisbie was following Nadine down the tower steps one morning when Nadine saw her "crowd against the spiral wall, slide down to the bottom, and fly into the living room."

Frisbie seemed to strongly feel the presence of the unseen Misty Friends in two of the second-floor rooms of the dwelling, and she entered those rooms only reluctantly. The Tugels used one of those rooms as their bedroom, and Nadine recalls the one day Frisbie followed her into the bedroom while she put away freshly laundered clothes. The cat was sitting on a chair attentively watching Nadine when "suddenly, for no apparent reason, Frisbie's hair bristled and she spit and hissed and flew out of the room like a streak. She sat in the hall waiting for me," says Nadine, "but she would not come back into the room."

Frisbie felt even more uncomfortable in the other upstairs room, the museum room—at least she felt uncomfortable in that room for the first two years she lived at the lighthouse. Every time she went into the museum room, she would cry to be picked up, recalls Nadine. And when Nadine was busy and couldn't pick her up, Frisbie would jump up on a bench or chair and wait for someone to hold her.

When Nadine talked with the daughter of one of Battery Point's former keepers, she learned that the museum room had been the woman's bedroom when she had lived in the dwelling. The woman told Nadine that when she was growing up she had sought "refuge in her bedroom during severe storms because she always felt the presence of the 'ghosts' there and they gave her a feeling of protection and safety."

Like the frightened young daughter of the former keeper, there came a time when Frisbie began to seek refuge in that special room. It started when she became very ill. "As sick as she was and obviously in great pain," remembers Nadine, "Frisbie would slip away from us and crawl up the stairway" to the museum/bedroom. "The fifth and last time ... she lay at the base of the Captain's portrait" and died. "Her actions ... seemed to show us that what she had feared so long, she now felt an affinity to," explains Nadine.

Two new little kittens soon found their way into Nadine's and Jerry's hearts—and into the keepers' dwelling at Battery Point. The Tugels appropriately named these two official new residents Captain Jeffrey and Captain Samuel, in honor of two men whose lives were closely linked to the lighthouse.

Captain John Jeffrey became the second keeper of Battery Point Lighthouse in 1875 and served for almost forty years. During those years, he became almost synonymous with the lighthouse—Battery Point was Captain Jeffrey's Lighthouse. The captain and his wife, Nellie, raised four children in this cozy dwelling perched on a 45-foot-high rocky outcropping at the end of Battery Point. Nellie must have had her hands full making sure her youngsters stayed in the yard and didn't slip into the seawater that completely surrounds the outcropping during all but low tide. The family usually timed their trips to the mainland to coincide with low tide, when they could walk across the relatively dry, rocky tidal passageway to Battery Point. The children went to school in Crescent City, and sometimes they would get caught on the mainland at high tide. Whenever that happened, Captain Jeffrey would have to launch the light station's boat and rescue his own children.

Captain Samuel DeWolf didn't live at Battery Point Lighthouse, but he died within sight of it. He went down with his side-wheel steamship, *Brother Jonathan,* when it crashed into treacherous St. George Reef during severe weather on July 30, 1865. Only nineteen of the almost 200 passengers and crew on board survived the shipwreck. Remnants of the ill-fated steamer now rest in the museum room at Battery Point Lighthouse.

Apparently, the Tugels' cats, Captain Jeffrey and Captain Samuel, like Frisbie before them, saw the Misty Friends and, like Frisbie, sometimes refused to go into a room at the lighthouse—or bolted from one for no apparent reason. Nadine reports that one evening when Jeffrey and Sam were "romping and rolling" in the living room, "Sam bristled, shot through the living room, the kitchen, and the screen door." Nadine explains that even though the door had well-secured heavy copper screening, Sam "went through it like it was made of tissue paper!" Nadine and Jerry caught up with Sam when he took refuge under the big water tank. It took them several hours to calm the badly frightened kitten.

Both Sam and Jeffrey obviously felt very uncomfortable in the radio room at Battery Point. One corner of the room in particular seemed to scare the cats—especially Sam. One evening when the gentle-natured Jeffrey was lying relatively peacefully on the radio room floor, "he suddenly tensed and slid backward," recalls Nadine. When Jerry reached down to pick him up, the frightened Jeffrey—who rarely extended his claws—clawed and scratched Jerry, all the while keeping his eyes glued on that one scary corner of the room. Jeffrey refused to venture back into the radio room for quite some time after that frightful evening.

Many of the keepers who have served at Battery Point Lighthouse during its 145-year history have reported unusual occurrences, including hearing footsteps in the tower during stormy weather. Usually the footsteps climb the tower stairs every hour on the hour as if someone were making doubly sure the light stayed lit to help mariners safely navigate the wind-driven waves and steer clear of St. George Reef.

Nadine tells about one stormy night when the footsteps in the tower woke up both the keeper and his wife. Even though the alarm had not rung to alert the keeper that the light had gone out, he had an eerie feeling that it had. He climbed the tower stairs to the service room, lifted the hatch, and looked up into the lantern room. Sure enough—the bulb had burned out. The keeper replaced the bulb and went back downstairs. Neither the keeper nor his wife heard the footsteps again that night, and when they checked the alarm the next day, they found it to be in perfect working condition. They never did figure out why the alarm hadn't gone off the night before, but if the phantom footsteps hadn't wakened them, the keeper would not have known the light had gone out.

One day a visitor came to the lighthouse and told Nadine, "I'll visit you during the day, but don't expect me to come out at night." The man went on to explain that he and a friend had once agreed to spend a night at the lighthouse, so the keepers could have some time off. Twice during the night the sound of organ music woke up both the man and his friend. After coming downstairs to the parlor the second time and finding no one in sight playing the organ, both men raced back upstairs, "threw their things into their bags, and nearly ran over each other on the way back to the mainland."

Nadine and Jerry never heard organ music, but they—and others—have heard voices in and around the lighthouse. Once, at about midnight, the sound of people talking woke up Nadine. She listened for awhile, and even though she couldn't make out the words, she could tell there were two distinct voices, one male and one female. Fearing that some unsuspecting couple had made their way from the mainland to the lighthouse in the dark and didn't realize how easily they could fall on the rocks, Nadine woke up Jerry. The two of them searched both the grounds and the lighthouse, but finding no one, they went back to bed.

About three o'clock that morning, Jerry woke up and heard the voices. This time the man and woman seemed to be inside the dwelling, in the Captain's room. Like Nadine, Jerry couldn't make out the words, but he did hear the woman giggle.

When Nadine and Jerry told their daughter, Deanna, about the voices they had heard, she more or less brushed it off. But one stormy, foggy night when Deanna and her daughter, Catrina, were visiting the lighthouse, Deanna suddenly turned to Nadine with an odd look on her face and asked, "What did you say, Mom?"

When Nadine replied that she hadn't said anything, Deanna asked Catrina the same question and got the same answer. Deanna explained that she had heard "someone speaking to her in a fleeting voice as they passed."

Later that evening when Nadine, Jerry, Deanna, and Catrina were watching television in the radio room, Jerry asked the others, one at a time, what they had said—and Nadine, Deanna, and Catrina replied they had said nothing. Like Deanna, Jerry had heard someone speaking to him.

Nadine also tells about the rocking chair that many people have seen rock by itself—and whenever the chair rocked, the distinct smell of pipe smoke filled the room. People got so tired of seeing the chair rock and smelling the pipe smoke that they banished the rocking chair to the basement. Nadine and Jerry rescued the chair and placed it in the Captain's room. Nadine says they never saw the chair rock, but she suggests the reason is because they did not spend much time in that particular room when they lived at the lighthouse.

Nadine and Jerry may not have seen the rocking chair move, but they know for sure that someone kept moving Jerry's slippers. Battery Point Lighthouse was relit as an active private aid to navigation in 1982, and the Tugels took their responsibility of keeping the light lit very seriously. Every evening Jerry deliberately placed his slippers next to his side of the bed where he could just slip into them in case the alarm sounded and he had to go up to the lantern room and replace the light bulb in the middle of the night. No matter how carefully Jerry positioned his slippers though, he would awake to find them pointing in the opposite direction! When he first accused Nadine of teasing him, she thought he was teasing *her* because she had not touched his slippers. Jerry finally just told Nadine to "quit moving them." Even though it was not Nadine, whoever was moving Jerry's slippers must have been listening because from that night on they always stayed right where he put them.

Evidently, the Misty Friends at Battery Point Lighthouse listened to Jerry on other occasions too and did what he told them. For instance, one day before Nadine and Jerry went to the mainland, they closed the door to the upstairs (so the cats couldn't get into the bedroom or museum room), locked the dwelling, and set the burglar alarm. When they came back late that evening, everything was just as they had left it—except when they climbed into bed, Nadine noticed a fairly large toasty-warm spot right by her feet. When she told Jerry about it, he said, "Well, why didn't they warm my side?" The next night the Tugels found another warm spot on the bed—this time on Jerry's side.

Another night, just after Nadine and Jerry had gone to bed, they felt an unexplainable thump. Jerry emphatically said to whoever was listening that he "wished they would leave us the privacy of our room." Nothing ever thumped the bed again.

Many people have speculated about the identity of the Misty Friends. During the 1960s a group from a school (no one recorded the name of the group or the school) spent some time poking around Battery Point Lighthouse and found evidence of the presence of three ghosts: two men and a child. One of the men may be Captain John Jeffrey—the old keeper may not have been willing to leave his lighthouse after taking such good care of it for almost forty years. Since there is no record of any children dying at the lighthouse, perhaps the child is one or more of Captain Jeffrey's children, lighthouse "brats" who, like their father, refuse to leave their lighthouse. The second man may be Captain Samuel DeWolf who would be particularly concerned that the light be kept burning to prevent other mariners from going down with their ships on the rocks of St. George Reef.

As Nadine says in her booklet, "There are many questions about the [ghostly] happenings, and we may never have the answers." She also says that she didn't write down the stories about the Misty Friends to "try to convince anyone that there are ghosts." She recorded the stories as a way of responding to the inevitable questions people ask about ghosts in the lighthouse.

After twelve years of service, Jerry and Nadine retired as the keepers of Battery Point Lighthouse in the mid-1990s. Don and Carol Vestal served as the keepers for two years, and in March 1998 Larry and Nancy

Schnider took up residence. The Schniders have been working hard to resurrect the history of the 150-year-old structure. Nancy emphasizes that they are focusing on restoring the historical authenticity of Battery Point Lighthouse.

The Schniders have borrowed antique furnishings from the Del Norte County Historical Society and brought up other old furnishings and artworks from the basement to restore the interior to its original 1850s appearance. Nancy says that now "visitors see nothing modern except the refrigerator." And when they give tours, Nancy, Larry, and the seventeen volunteer docents dress in period costumes, including old-fashioned high-top shoes for the women.

Nancy reports that she and Larry have placed the rocking chair in their bedroom, but they haven't seen it rock by itself. She suggests that the reason she hasn't experienced the Misty Friends is that she absolutely does not believe in them.

The Schniders—and probably the Misty Friends too—would enjoy having you visit them at Battery Point Lighthouse. Nancy and Larry promise that you really will feel like you are stepping back into time at this historic site. Just walking out to the lighthouse at low tide will give you a good feel for at least part of what it was like to serve as a keeper here.

When you visit Battery Point, you may want to go into the living room and stand in the doorway to the tower, where perhaps one of the Misty Friends will lightly touch you as if asking you to move out of the way. And after you courteously step aside, be sure to turn around to see who it was. Also spend some time in the bedroom watching the rocking chair. Perhaps you will see it rock by itself or smell the cigar smoke of the someone sitting in it. Perhaps by then Nancy will have changed her mind about the Misty Friends who keep her and Larry company at Battery Point Lighthouse.

Battery Point Lighthouse, which is maintained by the Del Norte County Historical Society, is open for tours April through September. The lighthouse stands on a rocky outcropping at the end of Battery Point, which is on the west side of the harbor at Crescent City in northern California. For more information, contact Del Norte County Historical Society, Battery Point Lighthouse, 577 H. Street, Crescent City, CA 95531; 707/464-3089.

At Cape Hatteras Lighthouse, the site of a mysterious tragedy, Theodosia Burr Alston walks the shore in search of her lost portrait. The actual circumstances of Theodosia's death remain unknown to this day.

Lovely Theodosia Still Walks the Beach Looking for Her Portrait

Cape Hatteras Lighthouse
on the Outer Banks, North Carolina

In an ironic twist of fate, Cape Hatteras Lighthouse united for all eternity three of the most prominent Americans of the late 1700s and early 1800s: U.S. Statesman and Secretary of the Treasury Alexander Hamilton, his political rival and dueling opponent U.S. Vice President Aaron Burr, and Burr's beloved daughter, Theodosia Burr Alston.

The fateful, convoluted tragedy begins with Hamilton, who recognized the economic need for our young nation to develop international trade. Hamilton played a key role in convincing the U.S. Congress to appropriate funds for lighthouse construction along the North Carolina coast, including Cape Hatteras to make shipping safer. Given the great congressional reluctance to spend money on navigational aids, Cape Hatteras Lighthouse may owe its very existence to Alexander Hamilton. As Charles Harry Whedbee wrote in *Legends of the Outer Banks and Tarheel Tidewater* (John F. Blair Publisher, 1966), Cape Hatteras Lighthouse was the direct result of Hamilton's lobbying, and it was sometimes called "Hamilton's Light."

Hamilton did not enjoy the same degree of success in lobbying for his point of view on issues with his contemporary, Aaron Burr, as he had with Congress about Cape Hatteras Lighthouse. Hamilton and Burr clashed time and time again in the political arena, and Hamilton doggedly opposed the ambitious Burr throughout his career as a statesman.

When Burr tied with Thomas Jefferson in the presidential election of 1800 and the task fell to the U.S. Congress to break the tie, Hamilton devoted every ounce of his energy to lobbying for Burr's defeat. It took thirty-six ballots, but Hamilton finally succeeded—and Congress elected Jefferson as the third President of the United States with Burr having to settle for the vice presidency.

Four years later when Burr ran for the office of governor of New York, Hamilton again did everything in his power to defeat him. After that second major defeat at Hamilton's hands, Burr would not rest until Hamilton agreed to meet him in a duel to the death. Burr mortally wounded Hamilton on July 11, 1804, on a "field of honor" in Weehawken, New Jersey. Hamilton died the following day—not quite a year after Cape Hatteras Lighthouse began active service and not quite ten years before Theodosia

Burr Alston sailed past Hamilton's Light on the final voyage of her life.

Theodosia both admired and adored her father. Burr's wife had died when Theodosia was still a child, and Burr had devoted himself to raising his daughter to be one of the most beautiful and well-educated young women of her day. He was pleased when she chose to marry an equally accomplished young man, Joseph Alston, from one of South Carolina's most prominent families. Soon after their marriage, Joseph was elected governor of South Carolina, a position that elevated both himself and Burr's daughter to the upper crust of American politics and society.

Theodosia and Joseph had one son, Aaron Burr Alston. No doubt the birth of his namesake grandson brought Burr much-needed joy in light of his political and personal demise since his duel with Hamilton. Public outcry over the fatal confrontation, coupled with the desire of his political opponents to undo him, had led to Burr's arrest and trial—not once, but twice—for treason. Although Burr was acquitted both times, he retreated to England in voluntary exile.

Burr returned to New York in 1812 when it became obvious that the English were planning to retake the colonies by force. Theodosia, who was most anxious to see her distraught father once he returned to New York, eagerly made travel plans. She and her son would sail from Georgetown, South Carolina, up the Atlantic Coast to New York Harbor. She just knew that seeing young Aaron—and the portrait of herself she had painted as a homecoming gift—would help lift her father's despair.

Before Theodosia embarked on her voyage to New York however, she suffered a heartbreaking tragedy of her own. Young Aaron Burr Alston contracted a fever, probably malaria, and died in June 1812. For the next several months, Theodosia retreated into a dark despair that bordered on insanity.

When Theodosia finally began to recover, Joseph convinced her to make the postponed voyage to New York to see her father. To ensure her safe passage through the British blockade along the East Coast, Joseph wrote an official letter as governor of South Carolina explaining Theodosia's mission and requesting that her ship, interestingly named the *Patriot,* be allowed to sail on to New York. He knew that out of courtesy to Theodosia and his governorship, the British officers aboard the warships would honor his request. The British did indeed honor the governor's request— the Outer Banks pirates did not.

Soon after the British detained and then courteously sent the *Patriot* on her way northward in the first days of January 1813, the little ship safely passed Cape Hatteras under the lifesaving beam of Hamilton's Light before running into heavy weather. The captain threw out a sea anchor (a drag probably made of canvas) to help keep the *Patriot* facing into the wind to slow drifting movement, and Theodosia and her shipmates waited out the storm.

In the 185 years since Theodosia embarked on her fateful voyage, various accounts have surfaced about exactly what happened to the *Patriot* once the storm subsided. In his book Whedbee reports that when the gale blew itself out the third night, the captain had no way of determining his ship's exact location. But almost miraculously, the light from what appeared to be a ship anchored nearby appeared. The captain ordered the *Patriot* to run full-speed toward it, hoping the other ship's captain could tell him where they were.

But what the *Patriot's* captain thought was the light of another ship turned out to be a lantern tied to the neck of a horse being led by a pirate along the beach— a trick used quite often in those days to lure ships too close to shore. The *Patriot* had already sailed into the breakers before the captain and crew realized they had been had—as so many other unsuspecting mariners had been before them—by the pirates of Nags Head.

As Whedbee tells the story, the pirates swarmed aboard the *Patriot* and ruthlessly murdered the entire crew, including Theodosia's personal maid. Seeing and hearing the horror around her, Theodosia once again retreated into insanity, a condition that the pirates for their own reasons respected. Perhaps fearing some instant and violent retribution from God, the pirates did not harm Theodosia but took her ashore with the one possession she had in her hands at the time—the portrait she was taking to her father in New York.

In the following years, according to Whedbee, the Nags Head pirates and fishermen and their families provided the childlike Theodosia with shelter, food, and whatever else she needed. She reportedly told everyone she met that she was on her way to visit her father in New York. The portrait Theodosia was taking to her father hung over the mantel in one of the cottages where she frequently stayed during the years she spent on the Outer Banks. When Theodosia had grown old and was ill, Dr. William G. Poole from Elizabeth City treated her whenever he visited the Outer Banks. And every time he did, he admired her portrait.

One stormy evening Dr. Poole gave Theodosia a sedative and then started to leave. The fisherman who owned the cottage tried to give him Theodosia's portrait in repayment for all he had done to help her. Before the doctor could accept the gift, Theodosia leaped from her bed, snatched away the portrait, and ran out into the storm. Whedbee reports that Theodosia's body was never found, but her portrait washed up on shore close to where she had disappeared. Dr. Poole took the painting back to his home in Elizabeth City, where people, including members of the Burr family, identified it as a portrait of Theodosia Burr Alston, who had been presumed lost at sea in 1813.

The story of Theodosia's portrait ran in a number of newspapers, and, according to Whedbee, three old former pirates made deathbed confessions about the role they had played in tricking the captain of the *Patriot* and killing everyone on board except the lovely, child-like Theodosia. Dr. Poole displayed the lovely portrait in his home, and after his death it eventually— ironically—made its way to Macbeth Art Gallery in New York, many years after Theodosia had set out to take it to her father there.

In *Incredible Mysteries and Legends of the Sea* (Dodd, Mead and Co., 1967), Edward Rowe Snow gives a slightly different account of what happened to the *Patriot,* Theodosia, and her portrait. Snow reports that Captain Dominique You, pirate Jean Lafitte's former second mate, pursued and overtook the storm-battered *Patriot* the morning after the wind and rain subsided. Captain You and his pirate band killed everyone on board, including Theodosia, and then ransacked the ship. They took some valuables but left behind

Theodosia's portrait and trunk of clothes. The next day wreckers boarded the sinking ship at Nags Head and managed to salvage a number of items, including Theodosia's portrait and trunk, before the *Patriot* went to the bottom.

According to Snow, a wrecker named Mann gave the portrait and trunk and some other salvaged items to his sweetheart, Lovie Tillet. Lovie kept Theodosia's possessions but left Mann for a rival suitor, John Wescott. Many years later Dr. William Gaskins Pool (probably the Dr. William G. Poole in Whedbee's account) treated Lovie when she fell ill. Dr. Pool saw and admired Theodosia's portrait when he went to Lovie's cottage, and after Lovie recovered she gave it to him. Just as in Whedbee's account, Dr. Pool displayed the portrait in his home, and after his death, it passed to family members and then to a museum.

Despite Whedbee's and Snow's accounts, Theodosia evidently believes the portrait she was taking to her father in New York is still missing because she has often been seen searching for it along the shore near Hamilton's Light. If you want to help Theodosia,

Historic Cape Hatteras Lighthouse continues to warn mariners to keep a safe distance from shore, but the ferocious storms that hit this area have driven many vessels off course and into deadly Diamond Shoals. When you visit Cape Hatteras, you will see the remnants of many shipwrecks—and you may also see a lovely lady who presumably lost her life here many, many years ago.

go to Cape Hatteras on an overcast day and walk up the beach toward Nags Head. When you see the child-like woman in old-fashioned dress, tell her as convincingly as you can that she can stop looking—her lovely portrait was found and was taken to New York many, many years ago.

Theodosia is not the only ghost you will encounter on the beach near Cape Hatteras. You will undoubtedly stumble upon the ghostly remains of some of the thousands of ships that unhappily ended their voyages on Diamond Shoals, the "graveyard of the Atlantic."

Perhaps the most famous shipwreck, the five-masted schooner *Carroll A. Deering,* ran aground sometime during the night of January 30, 1921. Coast guardsmen from four lifesaving stations made their way to within a quarter mile of the stranded vessel but could get no closer because of the rough surf and strong tides. When the lifesavers finally were able to board the schooner, they found no one on board. (Some accounts report that the lifesavers found one or two cats on the vessel and rescued them.) Wreckers salvaged what they could, and after a storm three weeks later, the heavily damaged ship was dynamited. For a while part of the bow from the *Carroll A. Deering* rested onshore at Ocracoke, but a hurricane later dislodged it and swept it ashore near Cape Hatteras Lighthouse.

For many years people have feared Cape Hatteras Lighthouse itself might succumb to the sea as the wind and waves erode more and more of the beach around its foundation. For current information on efforts to preserve this historic lighthouse, visit the Outer Banks Lighthouse Society Web site at www.outer-banks.com/lighthouse-society.

Cape Hatteras Lighthouse is maintained and operated by the National Park Service. For up-to-date information on when the tower and keepers' dwelling are open for tours and for information about visiting the Outer Banks, call 252/995-4474, the Dare County Tourist Bureau at 877/629-4386, or the Outer Banks Chamber of Commerce at 252/441-8144.

To reach Cape Hatteras Lighthouse turn off North Carolina Highway 12 on the Outer Banks at Buxton and follow the signs to the lighthouse. You will see the tower from the highway.

For firsthand stories from Rany Jennette and Wayland Baum, who lived at Cape Hatteras Lighthouse during the early part of the 1900s, see *Lighthouse Families* by Cheryl Shelton-Roberts and Bruce Roberts (Crane Hill Publishers, 1997 and 2006).

The Friends of Seguin Island are restoring the light station and invite you to come stand watch here in the summer. While you scan the horizon for passing ships, you may hear piano music, and if you listen carefully, you will realize you are hearing the same song over and over and over again.

Piano Music and the Sound of a Bouncing Ball Fill the Keeper's Dwelling

Seguin Island Lighthouse on Seguin Island off the Atlantic coast near Georgetown, Maine

One of the nineteenth century keepers at Seguin Island Lighthouse loved his wife so much that he went to the trouble of floating a piano across the three miles from the mainland to the island and wrestling it up the long, steep tramway to the dwelling. And his wife loved playing the piano so much that she played it for hours on end. But she had only one piece of music, which she played over and over again, hour after hour.

Sometimes too much of something, even something as lovely as well-practiced piano music, can turn a good thing into a bad thing. And that's exactly what happened at Seguin Island, according to a story that has been circulating for more than a hundred years. Evidently feeling like he couldn't stand to listen to another piano note for as long as he lived, the keeper reportedly grabbed an ax and used it to silence the piano once and for all. Unfortunately he didn't stop there. After axing the piano, the keeper axed his wife and then himself.

But perhaps the distraught keeper didn't succeed in silencing the piano—or killing his wife and himself—once and for all. Other keepers, including U.S. Coast Guardsmen who lived at the station in the 1970s and 1980s, as well as people on the mainland and fishermen and mariners passing the island, have reported hearing piano music on Seguin Island. And ever since the unfortunate incident, numerous people have reported seeing the old keeper and his wife at the light station.

Susan Wren Perow, who grew up on the mainland near Seguin Island and spent several months as lighthouse caretaker in 1990 and as museum curator in 1993, has not uncovered any historical data to support the story about the ax-wielding keeper. But she definitely understands how living on Seguin Island in the 1800s could have driven both the keeper and his wife insane with—or without—a piano and only one sheet of music.

In a 1994 article in the Bath, Maine, *Times Record,* Susan said that the summer caretakers who have stayed on the island since 1990 had "all remarked on occasional feelings of isolation." Susan suggested that without radios, telephones, or televisions to connect them with the people in the outside world, the keepers and their families who manned this light station in the nineteenth century would have suffered even more from feelings of isolation and loneliness. The heavy gray fog that frequently shrouds the island and the moans of the foghorn, which sounds more than thirty percent of the year, intensifies the sense of desolation at Seguin.

Susan also says that people "always think [they] hear voices on Seguin," perhaps because the baleful cries and caws of the thousands of gulls that nest on the island each spring and summer "almost sound like a human wail." But one evening during the July 4th weekend of 1993, when Susan was filling in for the lighthouse caretakers, she heard human voices in the keeper's dwelling. She had gone to bed early but was awakened by the sound of people talking. After checking around both inside and out, Susan realized that the voices were coming from her marine radio, which she was sure she had turned off before going to bed. Susan turned off the radio and went back to bed—only to have the voices wake her up again an hour later. She turned off the radio once more and went back to bed. Susan woke up three more times that night hearing voices, and she turned off the radio three more times before it finally stayed off.

William O. Thomson, historian, author, and the producer of a video called *New England's Haunted Lighthouses,* reports that some of the coast guardsmen stationed at Seguin heard someone coughing somewhere in the dwelling when all of them were in the same room and none of them had a cold. Other people swear they have heard a little girl laughing at times when there was no child in sight.

Susan's research has turned up reports of one of the keepers and his family drowning when their ship wrecked off the south side of the Seguin Island. Ever since that tragic accident, the keeper's wife is said to walk the cliffs and call out to her children in the churning water below. The little girl who can be heard laughing and sometimes seen in the dwelling may be one of the children who drowned, or she may be another keeper's daughter who died in her bedroom upstairs at the lighthouse in the late 1880s. People who have seen the little girl also have reported hearing the sound of a ball bouncing in the upstairs room.

Some of the coast guardsmen who have lived at the station in the past heard furniture moving around upstairs and doors slamming when all the official residents were sitting and accounted for in one of the downstairs rooms. A number of times jackets have fallen off hooks on the walls of the keeper's dwelling and tools have moved seemingly all by themselves.

Many people have reported hearing the old keeper's heavy footsteps as he climbs the spiral metal staircase in Seguin Island Lighthouse. Some people, including a few coast guardsmen, have actually seen the old keeper in the tower and in the dwelling. Once he was seen standing behind a man who was playing a game of checkers.

A short time after Seguin Island Lighthouse was automated a coast guardsman had a rather disconcerting encounter with the old keeper—or with perhaps another old-timer who for one reason or another refuses to leave his post. The coast guardsman and some others had made an overnight trip to the island to pack up the government-issued items that remained in the dwelling and transport them to the mainland. In the middle of the night, a keeper dressed in an oilskin coat and pants woke up the coast guardsman by shaking his bed. The keeper pleaded with him to leave the furniture and other items there, and for the coast guardsmen to leave his home alone. The shaken coast guardsman ran from the bedroom and spent the rest of the night in a room with another member of the work crew. The next day when the crew had loaded the furnishings and started to lower them down the tram to the dock, the chain on the tram broke, sending all the furnishings hurtling down the tracks and into the water.

In 1989 the Coast Guard leased the light station buildings and grounds to Friends of Seguin Island, a nonprofit organization dedicated to preserving and maintaining this historic site, including its buildings, artifacts, and environment. For the past twenty years volunteers have been working to restore the buildings to their original appearance, hopefully just the way the old keeper wants his lighthouse to be. The organization hired Susan to help create the historical museum now housed in the dwelling, and in August 1995 the group hosted a gala celebration of the lighthouse's 200th anniversary.

The Friends of Seguin Island heartily invite you to come to the island during the summer and experience for yourself what it was like to stand watch at this light station, which was commissioned by President George Washington himself. Be sure to climb the tower that rises almost 200 feet above the sea for one of the best views of the Maine coastline, and also visit the museum in the restored keepers' dwelling.

Perhaps while you are visiting Seguin Island, you will sense the old keeper on the tower stairs or hear someone playing the piano or see a little girl wave at you. Don't be afraid. These longtime residents have been nice to Susan and the others who have come to their lighthouse, and chances are they'll be nice to you too—just as long as you don't try to take away their furniture!

Seguin Island lies about 3 miles from the mouth of Kennebec River off the coast of Maine near Georgetown and Popham Beach. Maine Maritime Museum schedules several trips to the island each summer; call 207/443-1316 for more information.

For more information about Seguin Island Lighthouse contact Friends of Seguin Island, Box 866, Bath, ME 04530; 207/443-4808.

Visitors to Seul Choix Point Lighthouse will notice how peaceful and quiet it is on the shore of Lake Michigan in the Upper Peninsula. The captain of one Great Lakes ship evidently found such welcome refuge at Seul Choix Point that he decided to stay—permanently.

A Cigar-Smoking Prankster Stays One Step Ahead of the Docents

Seul Choix Point Lighthouse on Lake Michigan near Gulliver, Michigan

The Lake Michigan shoreline on the southern coast of Michigan's Upper Peninsula offers very few safe harbors. Early French explorers often found welcome refuge from the lake's sudden, violent storms in the harbor protected by a rocky peninsula they named Seul Choix ("SIS Shwa"), which means "only choice." James Townshend, the captain of a Great Lakes ship, found the harbor at Seul Choix Point so welcoming that he made it his port of choice for all eternity.

Captain Townshend probably dropped anchor at Seul Choix Point Lighthouse whenever he was sailing near this peninsula in northern Lake Michigan, not only to find refuge in stormy weather but also to visit his brother, Joseph, who was the keeper. In the mid-1990s when Marilyn Fischer, president of the Gulliver Historical Society, and genealogist Florence "Alex" Meron were researching the history of the light station, they found an old newspaper clipping that described some of the events that occurred during the captain's last visit to Seul Choix Point Lighthouse.

The captain was in his mid-sixties at the time, and according to the newspaper account, he suddenly fell seriously ill. Joseph made his ailing brother as comfortable as possible in the bedroom right at the top of the stairs in the keeper's dwelling. Joseph also undoubtedly did all he could to relieve his brother's suffering, but evidently to no avail. As lighthouse docents told videographer Rand Shackleton, who recently visited Seul Choix Point Lighthouse, Captain Townshend's "violent" illness caused him excruciating pain, and he screamed out in agony day and night.

Captain James Townshend died on August 12, 1910. His body was embalmed in the basement of the keeper's dwelling and then placed in a rough-hewn cedar casket for public viewing. The open casket stood in the parlor of the keeper's dwelling for a "long period of time"—perhaps to give the captain's family and friends a chance to reach the relatively isolated Seul Choix Point by ship or horse and buggy. His children reportedly traveled overland to Gulliver from Marquette, and "many visitors and friends came by boat to attend the funeral."

After paying her respects to the old captain and his family, one lady told a newspaper reporter that they had placed "copper pennies on his closed eyes to keep them shut." This lady evidently knew the captain before he died because she was able to describe some of his personal traits. She noted that the captain was a "very heavy cigar smoker."

In recent years Captain James Townshend's heavy cigar smoking has become a dead giveaway to his continuing presence at Seul Choix Point Lighthouse— even though his body was buried almost ninety years ago in a cemetery at Manistique. The old captain had the keeper's dwelling pretty much to himself for a while, once the U.S. Coast Guard automated the 1895 lighthouse in the 1970s. They removed the Fresnel lens and replaced it with an airport-style beacon that requires very little maintenance, eliminating the need for a resident keeper.

Members of the Gulliver Historical Society probably disrupted Captain Townshend's eternal rest when they started restoring the interior of the dwelling. In her October 1995 article titled "Ghost of the Seul Choix Point Lighthouse," Marilyn Fischer said that workmen "flatly refused to work in the upstairs' bedrooms" because they "felt the presence of something supernatural up there!"

Marilyn also reported that a carpenter, who was nailing down subflooring at the base of the oak staircase that leads to the second floor, heard the "distinct sounds of footsteps walking across the wooden floor in the rooms just above him." At first he thought the footsteps were just echoes from his hammering, because when he stopped hammering, the footsteps stopped. But after hearing the footsteps several more times, even though they corresponded with his hammering, the carpenter double-checked to make sure the doors were locked. Although he didn't actually go upstairs, he did call out, "Who's there?"

Assuring himself that he was the only person in the building at the time, the carpenter resumed his hammering. But this time when he stopped hammering, the footsteps continued—"heavy footsteps walking from bedroom to bedroom upstairs." Without doing any further investigating, the carpenter packed up his tools and left, "vowing never to return by himself."

A woman who was helping plan a wedding at the keeper's dwelling didn't hear Captain Townshend's footsteps, but she did feel his presence and smell his cigar smoke. Marilyn says the woman was sitting on a windowsill in the parlor looking at the staircase and trying to decide where to place the flowers, candles, and other decorations for the ceremony when she felt a "sudden bone-chilling coldness" and smelled strong, "pungent" cigar smoke.

The eerie sensations passed in a minute or two, and the brave woman searched the dwelling inside and out, going so far as to smell the furniture and items in closets, to find out what had caused the sudden rush of cold air and the cigar smoke. Finding no other living soul and no source of smoke, the woman returned to the parlor and sat down once more on the windowsill—and once more she felt a sudden coldness "as if someone had just opened a freezer locker" and was enveloped in pungent cigar smoke. Although the sensations passed just as quickly the second time as they had the first, the woman left the dwelling in haste.

Volunteer docents Avonda Rehs and Mary Carlson smelled strong cigar smoke in the dwelling one Saturday morning when they were greeting visitors and manning the gift shop. They quickly checked all around to make sure no one was smoking inside the building, but they found no smokers—at least no smokers they could see.

Avonda says she forgot all about smelling the smoke until later that morning when a woman visitor went upstairs to see the bedrooms and remarked loud enough to be heard downstairs, "I can smell strong cigar smoke up here." Avonda turned to Mary and said, "See, we're not the only ones!"

Bob Williams, a clairvoyant, has visited the keeper's dwelling at least twice to help the members of the historical society find out more about the cigar smoker who seems to have taken up residence in the keeper's dwelling. Bob strongly felt Captain Townshend's presence just inside the doorway to one of the second-floor rooms. And when he lifted his arms and reached toward the trapdoor to the attic just inside the doorway, he felt the chill of the captain's presence even more. Based on Bob's observations, the members of the historical society think that Captain Townshend hides in the attic when people are around and comes down when he thinks he has the house to himself.

And when Captain Townshend does come down out of the attic, he seems to like to play pranks. Avonda says that he sometimes turns over the silverware on the table (Captain Townshend used to hold his fork upside down when he ate). Once in a while the old captain shuts the Bible that's on display in the dwelling, and he seems to take great pleasure in turning the hat around on the mannequin that's dressed in an official keeper's uniform. Occasionally, Captain Townshend even puts a cigar or two in the pocket of the keeper's coat!

Sometimes Avonda and the other docents catch a glimpse of the old captain when they are cleaning the mirror on the dressing table upstairs in the dwelling. His face appears—Avonda says he has heavy eyes and a white beard—and his eyes follow the docents as they move about the room.

The members of Gulliver Historical Society have worked hard to restore and preserve Seul Choix Point Lighthouse, and they welcome you to come visit them—and Captain Townshend—to find out what it was like to serve as a keeper at this century-old light station. The society is currently producing a video about this historic tower that has helped many captains find refuge from Lake Michigan's sudden, violent storms—and perhaps they will catch old Captain Townshend trying to stick a cigar or two in the pocket of the light-keeper's coat!

If you visit Captain Townshend at Seul Choix Point Lighthouse, you may get to see some of the old captain's pranks.

When you visit Seul Choix Point Light Station, be sure to go upstairs in the dwelling and stand under the trapdoor leading to the attic and look in the mirror over the dressing table—maybe you too will feel the old captain's presence or catch a glimpse of his face. With more than 13,000 visitors coming to his dwelling each year, he's probably getting more and more used to getting less and less eternal rest.

Seul Choix Point Lighthouse stands at the end of the peninsula just southeast of Gulliver in Michigan's Upper Peninsula. Take U.S. 2 along the south coast of the Upper Peninsula to Gulliver and turn onto Port Inland Road. About 4 miles down the road turn right onto County Road 431 and follow the signs to the historic lighthouse.

You can explore the grounds year-round, weather permitting, and visit the two maritime museums (one in the restored dwelling and one in the fog-signal building) from Memorial Day through early October. For more information, call 906/283-3183.

Local residents rescued Old Port Boca Grande Lighthouse from falling into the Gulf of Mexico and then worked hard to restore the historic structure's former glory—which undoubtedly has made the little girl who lives here very happy. When you visit the museum, see if you can hear her bouncing a ball upstairs.

A Little Girl Sometimes Plays Upstairs in the Keeper's Dwelling

Old Port Boca Grande Lighthouse
on Gasparilla Island in the
Gulf of Mexico, Florida

M arilyn Hoeckel, the director of the Boca Grande
Lighthouse Museum/Interpretive Center, prefers
to talk about the restoration and preservation
projects going on at Old Port Boca Grande rather than
about the ghostly goings-on at the historic site.

And for sure, the history of Old Port Boca Grande
Lighthouse is rich enough without the added poignancy
of the little girl who has been playing upstairs in the keeper's dwelling for quite a number of years now. Or the
tragic romance of the Spanish princess who sometimes
walks along the beach at the end of Gasparilla Island.

The history of this Gulf Coast lighthouse already includes more than enough poignancy and romance. Against incredible odds, the 108-year-old wooden structure has continued to remain standing on its metal stilts despite the high tides and severe beach erosion that have threatened to topple it and despite the vandals who attacked it when the U.S. Coast Guard abandoned the historic structure in the mid-1960s. Local residents came to the rescue of this venerable lady and fought hard to save her from further damage by claiming her as their own. In 1972 they succeeded in having federal officials turn over ownership of the property to local authorities. And in 1980 they succeeded in having their lighthouse placed on the National Register of Historic Places.

But these lighthouse champions didn't stop there. After the Gasparilla Island Conservation and Improvement Association raised $50,000, which the Florida Department of Natural Resources matched, volunteers began the massive job of restoring Old Port Boca Grande Lighthouse. They worked hard, and by November 1986 they had restored much of the lady's former glory. The U.S. Coast Guard added the crowning touch when it reinstalled the original Fresnel lens in the lantern room and relit the lighthouse on November 21, 1986, returning Old Port Boca Grande Lighthouse to active service.

But the lighthouse's champions didn't stop there either. In 1989 the residents formed the Barrier Island Parks Society and undertook the project of establishing a museum in the restored keeper's dwelling.

But what about the little girl who has been seen playing in the keeper's dwelling? When pressed for more information about her, Marilyn acknowledges that the daughter of one of the keeper's did die in the dwelling, most likely of diphtheria or whooping cough. Annmarie Sampley, a former park ranger who led tours of the lighthouse, often pointed to a doorway on the second floor and told visitors that it was one of the little girl's favorite places to play. Annmarie would then add: "They say at midnight you can hear her play."

As for the Spanish princess, Marilyn doubts there is any basis for her romantic story. According to a time-honored legend, the infamous Spanish pirate Jose Gaspar, better known in Florida as Gasparilla, buried his treasure in the sands near where Old Port Boca Grande Lighthouse was built some ninety years later. In addition to jewels and gold and other riches, Gasparilla collected beautiful women and held them captive on the small island he called Cautiva, known today as Captiva, a few miles south of Gasparilla Island.

One day in the very early years of the nineteenth century, Gasparilla captured a Spanish princess named Josefa. Of all the beautiful women the pirate had captured, Josefa was the most beautiful—and the most determined not to let him have his way with her. According to the tragic legend, the more hopelessly Gasparilla fell in love with Josefa, the more forcefully she spurned him—until the day came that she'd had enough of the pirate's bold advances and spat in his face. Gasparilla instinctively reached for his sword and cut off Josefa's head, an impulsive act he immediately regretted.

Gasparilla tenderly gathered up Josefa's lifeless body and buried her in the sand on his island. Refusing to abandon her completely though, the brokenhearted, remorseful suitor allegedly carried his beloved's head with him for the rest of his days. And for many years after both Josefa and Gasparilla were dead, mariners and others reported seeing the headless Spanish princess wandering the beach on Gasparilla Island, presumably looking for her head.

When you visit Old Port Boca Grande Lighthouse, be sure to look at the exhibits in the museum and admire the beautifully restored historic building. As you walk through the rooms of the keeper's house, see if you can find any trace of the little girl who likes to play there. And as you walk the beach in front of the light-house, see if you can find any trace of the lovely Spanish princess who lost her head to a swashbuckling pirate long, long ago.

Old Port Boca Grande Lighthouse stands at the end of Gasparilla Island off the coast of Florida, northwest of Fort Myers. Take Exit 32 (Toledo Blade Boulevard) off I-75 to U.S. 41. Turn south onto Florida Highway 776 in Murdock, and then take Florida Highway 771 to Placida. Follow the signs to Boca Grande Causeway (a toll road) and Gasparilla Island.

Once you are on the island, follow the signs to Boca Grande and Old Port Boca Grande Lighthouse. You will reach Gasparilla Island Rear Range Light first; this steel skeletal tower is not open to the public, but you may want to stop at the public beach in front of it. Drive about 1 mile farther to the state park at the end of the island to see Old Port Boca Grande Lighthouse.

For more information about the lighthouse, call the Gasparilla Island State Park office at 941/964-1154.

In 1851 a young assistant keeper drowned while trying to keep the lamps burning in the original Minots Ledge Lighthouse—but that didn't stop him from continuing to warn mariners away from treacherous Cohasset Rocks. If you take a boat tour to the lighthouse, perhaps you will hear him calling out in his native Portuguese: "Keep away!"

The Forever-Young Assistant Keeper Warns Mariners Away from Cohasset Rocks

Minots Ledge Lighthouse off the coast near Scituate and Cohasset, Massachusetts

During the past 150 years, mariners approaching Boston Harbor from the south in heavy weather have reported seeing a young man in dripping wet clothes hanging on for dear life to the ladder at the bottom of Minots Ledge Lighthouse. Despite his precarious position, the young man sometimes frantically waves one arm as he shouts out in a foreign language.

The young man is believed to be Joseph Antoine, a Portuguese mariner who served as an assistant keeper at the original 1850 Minots Ledge Lighthouse. In *Guardians of the Lights* (Pineapple Press, 1995), Elinor De Wire says the first lighthouse looked like a "giant spider." Nine iron pilings, sunk into the submerged ledge and cemented into place, supported the keepers' dwelling and lantern room, which stood about seventy-five feet above the surface of the ocean. Captain William H. Smith designed this experimental structure to withstand high winds and storm-driven waves.

From the time the original lighthouse began active service on New Year's Day, 1850, Head Keeper Isaac Dunham noted that the waves passing through the iron legs made the tower shake and that the wind rocked it back and forth. Captain Smith assured Isaac that the skeletal-style lighthouse he had designed would stand firmly planted on Minots Ledge even if a hurricane hit it.

Still not convinced that the lighthouse was safe or sound, Isaac asked lighthouse officials to reinforce the tower's pilings. Before approving any funds for the project, the Lighthouse Service sent an inspector to independently evaluate the situation. Even though the inspector experienced firsthand how the wind and waves made the lighthouse reel like a drunken man, nothing was done to strengthen the structure. Isaac endured the nauseating tremors and swaying as long as he could. In October 1850, after ten months as head keeper, Isaac packed his bags, climbed down the ladder, and left Minots Ledge Lighthouse for a more stable assignment.

John Bennett succeeded Isaac and moved into the lighthouse's quarters with his two assistants, young Joseph Antoine and John Wilson. Head Keeper John Bennett, like Isaac Dunham before him, strongly urged lighthouse officials to reinforce the iron pilings, but again they did nothing.

Somehow the lighthouse and its keepers survived the winter storms of 1850, and on April 16, 1851, John Bennett rowed the lighthouse boat ashore to get much-needed supplies. While the head keeper was on the mainland, a storm suddenly blew in and made it impossible for him to return to the tower—which meant that his two assistants were stranded on Minots Ledge.

The head keeper watched in horror as the waves crashed over and around the lighthouse knowing all too well the horrendous shaking and swaying his two assistants were having to endure all by themselves in his absence. John Wilson and Joseph somehow managed to keep the light lit—until the lighthouse gave one last gut-wrenching shudder and toppled into the churning waters of the Atlantic.

When the head keeper looked out across the water toward Minots Ledge the morning of April 17, 1851, he saw no trace of the lighthouse. Joseph drowned, and his body washed ashore along with pieces of the destroyed lighthouse. John Wilson made it to shore alive but died of exposure before he was found.

The spirits of the two courageous assistant keepers, however, remained steadfastly on duty at their assigned post on Minots Ledge. When the existing replacement tower was completed in 1860, Joseph and John simply moved into the new lighthouse and resumed their job of warning mariners away from the underwater ledges and rocks that form the treacherous Cohasset Rocks. While both of them continue to stand watch and man the light, Joseph often goes the extra mile by climbing out on the tower's ladder and waving mariners off Cohasset Rocks, all the while shouting in his native Portuguese language, "Keep away! Keep away!"

The keepers who served at the new Minots Ledge Lighthouse, a much sturdier structure built of granite blocks locked together by dovetailing then cemented in place, reported a number of unexplainable helping-hands experiences. Joseph and John sometimes cleaned the lens and lamp in the lantern room, a favor their fellow assistant keepers greatly appreciated.

During the time Joseph and John served under Head Keeper John Bennett in the original lighthouse, they had used a tapping system to let the keeper on watch know that one of the others was on his way upstairs to relieve him. One night when one of the keepers in the new tower was about to go off duty, he tapped his pipe on a table in the watch room and was surprised to get an answering tapping from below. He guessed that his relief keeper was signaling that he was on his way upstairs. But when the relief keeper didn't show up, the other man rang the bell connected to the keepers' quarters, the usual signal that it was time for the new watch to begin. The keepers finally realized that Joseph and John were continuing to use their old tapping system while they were on duty in the new lighthouse.

At least one time the new keepers were most grateful for the alert presence—and tapping—of the former assistant keepers. The wind had picked up late that afternoon before the keepers had lit the lamp in the lantern room. When the keepers heard almost frantic, very loud tapping echoing throughout the tower, they knew something was wrong, and they raced upstairs to the lantern room. They found the door to the catwalk had somehow come unlatched and was swinging back and forth in the wind. They immediately secured the door and checked the lens and lamp for damage. Fortunately, there was no damage—but there might very well have been damage if the door had stayed open much longer.

Unlike its predecessor, the new Minots Ledge Lighthouse survived nor'easters and crashing tower-high waves for more than 120 years without toppling into the Atlantic. A $500,000 renovation project in the 1980s replaced the worn granite blocks with new ones, strengthening Minots Ledge Lighthouse for its next century of active service.

The light at Minots Ledge flashes in a distinct 1 + 4 + 3 pattern, which local residents interpret as I LOVE YOU. Some people call this lighthouse the I-LOVE-YOU Lighthouse, a most appropriate name. Minots Ledge Lighthouse says what lighthouses and their keepers have always told the people who see them: "I love you—I love you so much that I will lay down my life to save yours."

Minots Ledge Lighthouse embodies the lifesaving spirit of keepers everywhere. Standing firm on its submerged foundation, sending out its beam night after night no matter how hard the wind blows or how high the waves reach, Minots Ledge Lighthouse symbolizes courage, faithfulness, endurance, and strength. By day the tower itself and by night the flashing beam of light send out their welcoming and warning messages loud and clear: "I'll be waiting for you when you come back! Watch out for that rock! You're right on course! I'm here if you need some help! You can count on me! Welcome home!"

When you stand on the Massachusetts shore south of Boston and look out at Minots Ledge Lighthouse, or when you pass by it in a boat, think about Joseph Antoine and John Wilson. Remember how they courageously kept the light burning at the top of their "giant spider" of a lighthouse until the wind and waves pushed it—and them—off the ledge and into the ocean. And think about lighthouse keepers everywhere who, like Joseph and John, faithfully served others as long as they lived—and sometimes beyond.

Minots Ledge Lighthouse has stood empty since the U.S. Coast Guard automated the light in 1947, and it is not open to the public. You can see it from the Massachusetts shoreline near Cohasset and Scituate. The Scituate Historical Society offers narrated boat tours to the tower; for more information, contact Scituate Historical Society, P.O. Box 276, Scituate, MA 02066; 781/545-1083.

During the 1980s renovation, the original granite blocks from the lighthouse watch room were used to build a 26-foot-tall Minots Ledge Monument on Government Island in Cohasset Harbor north of North Scituate. You can also see Minots Ledge Lighthouse's beautifully restored 1,500-pound fog bell on Government Island. For more information, contact the Cohasset Lightkeepers Corporation, P.O. Box 514, Cohasset, MA 02025; 781/383-1433; or the Cohasset Historical Society at 781/383-1434.

When Keeper James Davis died, his wife, Ann, took over and continued to stand watch for thirty years at Point Lookout Lighthouse. Ann did an exceptionally good job—and may have remained at her post to make sure "her" lighthouse was taken care of properly. When you visit Point Lookout Lighthouse, see if you think the current conditions meet Ann's high standards.

A Diligent Keeper Still Stands Watch

Point Lookout Lighthouse near St. Mary's City, Maryland

Except for the short tower on top, it looks like the home of many other longtime Chesapeake Bay residents. The Maryland Committee for Psychic Research has confirmed that Point Lookout Lighthouse is indeed the home of many longtime residents. And a good number of them are still wearing their Civil War-era clothes.

That makes perfectly good sense, since the nightly sweep of the light in the tower of the house once illuminated two nearby Civil War sites: Camp Hoffman and Hammond General Hospital. Camp Hoffman served as a federal prisoner-of-war camp for Confederate soldiers. The federal government built the hospital here in 1862 to treat Union soldiers, but the doctors and nurses treated Confederates as well. Some of the thousands of prisoners and wounded Union and Confederate soldiers who spent their last hours under the lifesaving beam of Point Lookout's tower may very well have chosen to remain permanently within sight, or just within, the lighthouse.

Elinor De Wire describes a number of Point Lookout Lighthouse's Civil War-era and other longtime residents in *Guardians of the Lights* (Pineapple Press, 1995) and *Sentries along the Shore* (Sentinel Publications, 1997). One of them, believed to be Ann Davis, wears an ankle-length blue skirt and a white blouse. Ann's husband, James, served as the first keeper of the lighthouse when it was completed in the 1830s. Sadly, he died a short time later. After her husband's death, Ann assumed responsibility for keeping the lamp lit, the lens clean, the brass polished, and everything in topnotch, white-glove condition in both the keeper's quarters and the tower.

In 1840 the captain of a lighthouse supply ship noted in his report that Ann was a "fine woman" and he felt sorry that she had "to live on a small naked point of land." Evidently, Ann rather liked this point of land, which provides a sweeping panoramic view of the Chesapeake, because she served as keeper of Point Lookout Lighthouse for a total of thirty years. And it seems that even after three decades as keeper, Ann has continued to keep watch at Point Lookout. The keepers who followed her at the lighthouse, as well as visitors, often reported seeing Ann on the landing at the top of the stairs and hearing her sigh—perhaps because the current keepers weren't keeping the lighthouse up to her high standards.

Elinor reports that one of the rangers at Point Lookout State Park encountered another one of the lighthouse's nineteenth-century residents one stormy night in December 1977. The ranger met Joseph Haney, an officer from the steamer *Express.* Joseph had drowned near the lighthouse in 1878 during a heavy storm that was very similar to the one brewing that December night a century later in the same location. The ranger saw Joseph peering in the back door of the house, but when he opened the door to let him in, Joseph "drifted backward and seemed to disintegrate."

According to Elinor, this same park ranger had a number of other encounters with Point Lookout Lighthouse's old-time residents, and many of them didn't seem to care very much—if at all—if they bothered him with all their comings and goings and carryings-on. The ranger reported hearing doors opening and shutting, people talking, and heavy sleepers snoring. He also reported hearing footsteps and the rustle of clothing, and feeling the air move and the floor shake as a group of "people" walked past him in the kitchen one evening as they made their way into another room.

In the late 1980s Allan Goddard heard one of the lighthouse's residents open a door in the abandoned, "locked up tighter than a drum" dwelling. He and his boss had gone to the property, which is owned by the U.S. Navy, to test the water in the well to make sure it was safe for some navy personnel who were moving into an adjacent building. Allan had heard stories about Ann and the other old-timers who reportedly live in the lighthouse, and he wanted to get inside to see them for himself.

Allan tried to get in, but all the doors and windows were securely locked—to keep vandals out of the dwelling as well as other unauthorized personnel. The only door Allan and his boss could open led to the basement, where the well is located.

While Allan and his boss were working on the well, they heard a door creaking on the first floor of the dwelling above them. "Good," said Allan to his boss. "Let's go up and find who's upstairs, so we can get inside and see the tower."

They walked all around the building and again tried all the doors and windows, but they found no trace of any other living soul anywhere around the house or on the grounds. They knew it couldn't have been the wind blowing through the house that had made the door creak because there was no wind that morning. Not finding anyone or anything that could account for the noises they heard, the two men decided it was "time to leave!" Even though he hadn't actually seen them, Allan knows someone had been in the house that morning.

Allan, who lives near Point Lookout Lighthouse, ventured back to the dwelling—this time as part of a large group—for a Christmas-in-April cleanup day on April 27, 1996. About sixty-five volunteers spent the day scraping, priming, and painting the outside of the lighthouse and tower, as well as shaping up the yard.

No one reported hearing or seeing any of the lighthouse's residents that day. Perhaps they were staying out of everybody's way, so they wouldn't inadvertently interrupt the much-needed house cleaning. When the volunteer work crew left at the end of the cleanup day though, the lighthouse's residents, especially Keeper Ann Davis, must have been very pleased. Their home now looks every bit as good, maybe even better, than the homes of other longtime Chesapeake Bay residents. And Ann knows that at least the outside would pass a surprise white-glove visit from the lighthouse inspector!

The U.S. Coast Guard decommissioned Point Lookout Lighthouse in the mid-1960s and replaced it with an automated beacon on a skeleton tower. Point Lookout State Park offers open house tours of the lighthouse. Call 301/872-5688 to check dates and times.

From its cliff-top perch, Split Rock Lighthouse guides mariners along this dangerous coastline where iron ore makes compass needles swing widely back and forth. Head Keeper Orren "Pete" Young stood watch in the lantern room high above Lake Superior for the first time in 1910—and he may still be keeping watch. (See photo on page xii.)

The "Real" Keeper

Split Rock Lighthouse on Lake Superior near Two Harbors, Minnesota

When Lee Radzak invites you to explore life in the "past" lane at Split Rock Lighthouse, he definitely knows whereof he speaks—because Lee Radzak has been *living* life in the past lane at Split Rock Lighthouse for quite some time.

The U.S. Coast Guard decommissioned the lighthouse in 1969, which eliminated the need for a resident keeper. But Lee still gets up in the morning and puts on his circa-1910 Lighthouse Service keeper's uniform. And he lives in one of the three keeper's dwellings at the light station. And he keeps everything at his light station in perfect working order—which is exactly what the Lighthouse Service expected their employees to do.

But Lee isn't a Lighthouse Service employee—he's a Minnesota Historical Society employee. He's not really the head keeper of Split Rock Lighthouse, but he does serve as the site manager of the historic light station. Lee and the other historical society employees at Split Rock dress in authentic period clothing and give interpretive tours of the picturesque 1910 lighthouse, the fog-signal building, and a keeper's dwelling that has been restored to its 1920s appearance.

"Head Keeper" Lee Radzak and the other men and women who serve as docents lead visitors to the top of the tower and show them the huge clamshell lens in the lantern room. The docents point out across Lake Superior and tell about the intense blizzard that sent more than thirty vessels to the bottom of the lake along this rocky coastline on November 28, 1905. They explain that mariners sometimes have a hard time navigating along this coast because the iron in the nearby mountains makes compass needles swing widely back and forth, and the water is unusually deep at the base of the cliffs, which makes depth soundings unreliable.

The docents also describe how difficult it was to build a lighthouse atop the cliff at this remote site, which is accessible only from the water (see photo, page xii). Construction workers had to overcome incredible obstacles, and taxpayers had to spend more than $72,000 before the tower was completed. Orren "Pete" Young lit the lamp in Split Rock Lighthouse for the first time in 1910. Head Keeper Young continued to serve at Split Rock Lighthouse until 1928, when he retired at age seventy.

Or maybe Head Keeper Young didn't retire—maybe he decided he didn't want to give up the post he had held for so many years. Perhaps he decided to hang around Split Rock Lighthouse and continue his faithful watch, especially after the U.S. Coast Guard darkened his light and abandoned the buildings he had taken such good care of for almost two decades. And after his light station became part of Split Rock State Park and the Minnesota Historical Society restored the buildings, maybe the old head keeper decided to help keep the past alive at the light station.

Maybe it was Head Keeper Young a visitor saw in the lighthouse after hours one evening in the mid-1980s.

Thc docents at Split Rock Lighthouse wear authentic period costumes to help you "explore life in the past lane." As you climb the tower to the lantern room, take a close look at the costumed guides and see if you can spot the "real" keeper, the one wearing his own clothes.

After touring the tower that day, the visitor realized that his wallet was missing. He backtracked to the tower to look for it and knocked hard on the locked door, hoping that one of the docents was still inside.

As one version of the story goes, when no one responded to the man's knocking, he stepped back to see if one of the docents was still up in the lantern room. He saw an old man in a keeper's uniform on the catwalk outside the lantern room. As he was about to knock on the door again, the visitor noticed the door was padlocked from the outside. He wondered who the old keeper was and why he was in the locked tower. When the visitor returned to the lighthouse the next day, the docents gave him his wallet but couldn't tell him anything about the old man he had seen at the top of the tower.

In another version of the incident, the visitor pounded on the tower door for quite a long while, and the old keeper finally opened the door and handed him the wallet. When the visitor asked docents about the old man in the lighthouse, no one knew anything about him.

According to Frederick Stonehouse, the wife of the resident curator in the mid-1980s also encountered a person no one knew anything about. As Stonehouse reports in *Haunted Lakes* (Lake Superior Port Cities Inc., 1997), the curator's wife was in their bedroom in one of the keeper's dwellings one evening when she smelled very strong perfume and sensed that she was being watched. But no one else was in the room or anywhere else nearby, and none of the women docents wore strong perfume. Perhaps like Head Keeper Young, some longtime female resident has decided to stay on at Split Rock Lighthouse to help keep the past alive.

When you accept Lee Radzak's invitation to explore life in the past lane at this living-history museum, look carefully at the docents as you tour the lighthouse tower and the keeper's dwelling. See if you can figure out which docent is the real keeper and which one is the real keeper's wife. They'll be the ones who are wearing their very own clothes—not period costumes like the rest of the docents at Split Rock Lighthouse.

You can tour the tower, fog-signal building, and the restored keeper's dwelling at Split Rock Lighthouse from mid-May through mid-October. You can visit the facility's history center year-round to see an award-winning film and outstanding exhibits. For more information, call 218/226-6372 or visit www.mnhs.org. The light station stands in Split Rock Lighthouse State Park on U.S. 61 about 20 miles north of Two Harbors.

Either before or after you visit Split Rock Lighthouse, stop in Two Harbors to tour the 1892 Two Harbors Lighthouse, which stands at the tip of a spit of land that separates Agate and Burlington Bays. As ships became equipped with high-tech navigational instruments in the last half of the twentieth century, the need for lighthouses diminished and the U.S. Coast Guard began automating and then decommissioning many of these historic structures. Anticipating the day Two Harbors Lighthouse would be ruled unnecessary as an active navigational aid, the members of Lake County Historical Society had the light station listed on the National Register of Historic Sites.

This listing means that the fully automated lighthouse must remain in active service.

The Coast Guard continues to maintain the light at Two Harbors Lighthouse, and the historical society has opened the tower and assistant keeper's house to the public. In addition to the light station, the historical society operates the Edna G. Tugboat Museum, the Depot Museum, and the 3M Dawn Museum. For more information, call 218/834-4898.

From U.S. 61 in Two Harbors turn toward Lake Superior on Scenic Byway/First Street and follow the Scenic Byway along First Avenue to Third Street. Two Harbors Lighthouse stands on the lakeshore at the end of Third Street. You can also walk out on the nearby breakwater to get a close-up view of Two Harbors East Breakwater Lighthouse.

For More Information about Lighthouses

Cohasset Historical Society Maritime Museum
Minots Ledge Lighthouse
4 Elm Street
Cohasset, MA 02055

Del Norte County Historical Society
Battery Point Lighthouse
577 H Street
Crescent City, CA 95531

Friends of Seguin Island
Seguin Island Lighthouse
Box 866
Bath, ME 04530

The Great Lakes Historical Society
480 Main Street
Vermilion, OH 44089

Great Lakes Lighthouse Keepers Association
P.O. Box 219
Mackinaw City, MI 49701

Gulliver Historical Society
Seul Choix Point Lighthouse
672 N West Gulliver Lk. Rd.
Gulliver, MI 49840

Lighthouse Preservation Society
4 Middle Street
Newburyport, MA 01950

Massachusetts Chapter of the U.S. Lighthouse Society
314 Spring Street
Hanson, MA 02341

Minnesota Historical Society
Split Rock Lighthouse
3713 Split Rock Lighthouse Rd.
Two Harbors, MN 55616

National Archives
Record Group 26
Washington, DC 20480

American Lighthouse Foundation
P.O. Box 565
Rockland, ME 04841

Old Port Boca Grande Lighthouse
Gasparilla Island State Park
P.O. Box 1150
Boca Grande, FL 33921

Old Presque Isle Lighthouse and Museum
5295 Grand Lake Road
Presque Isle, MI 49777

Outer Banks Lighthouse Society
P.O. Box 1005
Morehead City, NC 28557

Scituate Historical Society
Minots Ledge Lighthouse
P.O. Box 276
Scituate, MA 02066

St. Augustine Lighthouse
81 Lighthouse Avenue
St. Augustine, FL 32080

Tybee Island Light Station
P.O. Box 366
Tybee Island, GA 31328

U.S. Coast Guard
Historian's Office (G-09224)
2100 Second Street Southwest
Washington, DC 20593

U.S. Lighthouse Society
244 Kearney Street, Fifth Floor
San Francisco, CA 94108

About the Authors

Author Norma Elizabeth Butterworth-McKittrick

Norma has worked as a book, magazine, and newsletter editor for more than fifteen years, including ten years with *Southern Living* and *Cooking Light* magazines and three years with Crane Hill Publishers. She assisted with the writing and research for several books, including *Plantation Homes of the James River* (The University of North Carolina Press) and *Steel Ships and Iron Men* (Globe Pequot Press). In 1997 she authored a children's book, a retelling of *The Nutcracker* with original illustrations by Anita Bice (Sweetwater Press).

Although Norma has edited and proofread a number of books about lighthouses, this is the first book she has written about them. Norma lives in Birmingham, Alabama.

Photographer Bruce Roberts

Bruce, a former director of photography and senior photographer for *Southern Living* magazine, began his photo-journalism career at *The Tampa Tribune.* In the early 1960s he became one of the legendary *Charlotte* (North Carolina) *Observer* staffers. Bruce's photographs also have appeared in *Sports Illustrated, Time, Life,* and *Time Life Books.* Bruce has won numerous international, national, and state awards, and some of his photographs are in the permanent collection of the Smithsonian Institution.

Bruce coauthored *American Lighthouses* (Globe Pequot Press), a best-selling series of lighthouse guidebooks (Globe Pequot Press), and three popular historical books: *Plantation Homes of the James River* (The University of North Carolina Press), *American Country Stores* (Globe Pequot Press), and *Steel Ships and Iron Men* (Globe Pequot Press).

In 1997 Bruce and his wife, Cheryl Shelton-Roberts, coauthored the best-selling *Lighthouse Families* (Crane Hill Publishers). Bruce and Cheryl live in Morehead City, North Carolina.

Also from CRANE HILL PUBLISHERS

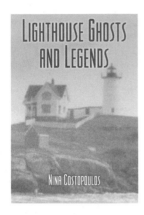

Lighthouse Ghosts
and Legends
1-57587-092-4

Lighthouse
Trivia
1-57587-169-6

Lighthouse
Families
1-57587-246-3